The present Master of Caius has had an unusual intellectual history. Trained in the biochemical school of Frederick Gowland Hopkins at Cambridge, he made his name with 'Chemical Embryology' and 'Biochemistry and Morphogenesis' as a scientific worker on the borderline of physiological chemistry and the morphological sciences. This was the field of work for which he was elected into the Fellowship of the Royal Society. And those were the years in which we published his books of essays 'Time, the Refreshing River' and 'History is on Our Side.'

But after several decades a new influence appeared in the form of certain young Chinese scientists who came to work with him and his colleagues in Cambridge; through them he acquired the beginnings of his knowledge of the language and culture of China. When the second world war made China and Britain allies, Joseph Needham was asked to lead a mission of scientific and technological liaison which gave him four years of life in China, ranging widely in the course of his work through most of the historic provinces. He was thus able to meet a host of Chinese scientists, engineers and doctors who were able to give him an orientation into the history of science and technology in their own culture; and he began to build up a unique working library of the Chinese books necessary for the writing of the work on this whole subject which he started when he returned to Cambridge in 1948. Since the communist revolution he has revisited China thrice, in 1952, 1958 and 1964. The Master of Caius is thus a man who has a right to speak about traditional Chinese culture, its present position, and its probable future development. In this book he reprints a number of addresses and lectures given from time to time during the past twenty-five years; but appropriately besides this (since all Chinese scholars have always been poets) he adds a number of poems which in his various periods of life in China he has on occasion felt moved to write.

WITHIN THE FOUR SEAS

℘ He who respects the dignity of man, and practises
what love and courtesy require—for him all men
within the four seas are brothers.

Lun Yü XII, v, 4

Conversations and Discourses
(of Confucius),
fifth century B.C.

WITHIN THE FOUR SEAS

THE DIALOGUE OF EAST AND WEST

Joseph Needham, F.R.S.

UNIVERSITY OF TORONTO PRESS

Toronto and Buffalo

FIRST PUBLISHED IN 1969
SECOND IMPRESSION 1979
Published in Canada and the United States by
University of Toronto Press
Toronto and Buffalo

PRINTED IN GREAT BRITAIN

UTP ISBN 0 8020 6360 8

PIPITULAE

meae
in laboratorio spagyrico
in terris sericis
in liturgio ecclesiae
in vitae peregrinatione

SYNERGUMENAE

DILECTISSIMAE

The system of romanization of Chinese names used in this book is that of Wade-Giles with *h* substituted for the aspirate apostrophe.

CONTENTS

THE DIALOGUE
OF EAST AND WEST

Adapted from the Presidential Address to
the Britain-China Friendship Association,
1955

For three thousand years a dialogue has been going on beween the
two ends of the Old World. Greatly have they influenced each
other, and very different are the cultures they have produced. We
have now good reason to think that the problems of the world
will never be solved so long as they are considered only from a
European point of view. It is necessary to see Europe from the
outside, to see European history, and European failure no less than
European achievement, through the eyes of that larger part of
humanity, the peoples of Asia (and indeed also of Africa).

PRIDE AND PREJUDICE

Many people in Western Europe and European America suffer
from what may be called spiritual pride. They are firmly convinced that their own form of civilization is the only universal
form. In deep ignorance of the intellectual and social conceptions
and traditions of other peoples, they think it quite natural to impose
upon them their own ideas and customary practices, whether of
law, of democratic society, or of political institutions. Yet they
propagate a culture which is somewhat self-contradictory, for
Europe has never fully succeeded in reconciling the material and
the spiritual, the rational and the romantic. And their way of life

tends to corrode and destroy those of neighbouring cultures, some of which may embody saner values.

Now the rise of modern science and technology in Western Europe, bringing in its train powers over nature previously unimaginable, has given Americans and Europeans an almost unconscious psychology of dominance. This mentality has been confirmed by the annexations, wars of conquest, and 'punitive expeditions' of the period of colonial expansion, so that today European-American values are offered, as it were, at the point of a Bren gun, with the atomic mushroom looming in the background. Christian civilization shows no better Christian humility today than it did at the time of the Crusades, when yet the civilization of Islam was on the whole a higher one than that of Europe. But a self-esteem then merely absurd is today a grave menace to all human beings.

UNIVERSALITY AND SUPERIORITY

It is sometimes said that European culture has a universal vocation, a superior creative dynamic activity, distinguishing it from all others. Its expansion is held to be the natural consequence of this 'superiority'. And Western European culture seems still to be spreading through the whole world, while other cultures remain local, and hard put to it to defend their territories.

Universality and superiority are comforting conclusions for Westerners to reach about themselves. Yet there is a fallacy in it. That the civilization of Europe did indeed produce the modern unified world entity of the aerofoil and the radio wave is a historical fact. But this was done not by lawyers, by theologians, by politicians, by writers; it was done by engineers and scientists. What must be asked, therefore, is which parts of modern 'European' world civilization are universal, and which parts are locally and parochially European? Once the question is rightly stated the answer is obvious. The real universal factors are modern science and modern technology, together with the philosophies which made them possible. And it should be clearly understood that

12

Europe did not give rise to 'European' or 'Western' science, but to universally valid world science.[1]

Now scientists and engineers of all races and peoples well understand each other whenever and wherever they meet; they speak the same language, they know the same truth. For Nature is no respecter of persons. All human beings, irrespective of race as of sex, given the training and the adequate qualification, are equal in the presence of the natural fact. And science is essentially a social undertaking. Observers of Nature form a world community. If I descend into the depths my brother is there also; if I fly up into the heavens, my pilot can be a Chinese, my co-pilot an Indian; my navigator an African. He that despiseth man despiseth not Man, but – Nature. This kind of mistake is not made with impunity.

The basic fallacy of Europocentrism is therefore the tacit assumption that because modern science and technology, which grew up indeed in post-Renaissance Europe, are universal, everything else European is universal also.[2] Roman law is 'obviously'

[1] It is extremely interesting that this distinction was appreciated by the Chinese from the very beginning of the introduction of modern science from Europe by the Jesuits. About 1640 there was discussion in Peking as to whether the new sciences were primarily 'Western' or primarily 'New'. The Jesuit missionaries wanted the accent to be on the Western origin because the religion which they propagated was Western in Chinese eyes, and their aim was to support and commend it by the prestige of the science which accompanied it. But the Chinese objected to the word 'Western' used by the Jesuits in the titles of the scientific books which they wrote and translated; and in 1669 the Khang-Hsi emperor finally insisted that it should be dropped in favour of 'New'.

[2] Some eminent European scholars say that modern science and technology, in their victorious spread throughout the world, have been accompanied by a mutilated secularized form of European civilization. And they note with distress that the European religious values have been decisively rejected by all Asian and African movements of national independence. For these scholars regard the civilization of Christendom as formally inseparable from the modern scientific view of the world; the necessary concomitant of the latter. From this it might be but a step to the preaching of a new crusade to impose fuller forms of European religion upon the rest of the world. Crosses might figure on its banners, but needless to say, capitalism and imperialism would carry them. Exactly what philosophy is the necessary accompaniment of modern science and technology has never yet been adequately formulated, though the problem has been in the minds of all the great Chinese reformers and revolutionaries for the past hundred

the greatest achievement of the human mind in jurisprudence, Greek philosophy (it goes without saying) the nearest approach to metaphysical truth ever attained by humanity, our own religion (with all its most minor accidents of time, place, and theory) revealed truth incumbent upon all men everywhere to believe. European painting and sculpture is 'absolute' painting and sculpture; that which artists of all other cultures must have been trying unsuccessfully to attain. European music is music; all other music is anthropology. And what is good enough (in cinema, reading-matter, or way of life) for the European (or American) man in the street, must be good enough for everybody.

Drastic revision of these unspoken assumptions is urgently necessary. The view often put forward that Western European civilization alone has produced a true historical sense is quite inadmissible. If any civilization were to be chosen for this honour it should be that of the Chinese, whose twenty-four dynastic histories, from 90 B.C. onwards, constitute a state-supported (but largely independent) corpus of historical writing unapproached elsewhere in the world. This is to say nothing of the lesser, though still very great, compilations such as the *Tzu Chih Thung Chien* (eleventh century A.D.) and the *Wên Hsien Thung Khao* (fourteenth century A.D.). Even if the term 'historical sense' be taken to mean 'philosophy of history', the European contributions were not the earliest. Ibn Khaldun lived some three centuries before Vico. Again, in philosophy, the ideas that in Chinese thought 'celestial immobility' was the supreme value, and that this corresponded with a 'static' quality of Chinese civilization, are both quite indefensible. The 'unmoved mover' was an essentially Greek idea; the Chinese conception of the Tao implied constant and unceasing activity, as in the apparent diurnal revolution of the stars. Of course instances of both kinds of valuation of rest and motion can be found in both civilizations. There was never anything static about Chinese civilization, except that (a) it proved capable of having a

---

years. Chinese scholars of the present day would certainly point to dialectical materialism as the answer. The Far West has not so far offered any serious alternative.

longer continuous history of recognizable identity as to language and culture than any other has been able to show (with the possible parallel of Israel), and (b) it did not produce any social phenomenon comparable to that of the European Renaissance with all its concomitant and following changes. There were in China periods of rapid advance and periods of relative quiescence, as in all other cultures.

Europeans must realize today that they should share with their brothers of Asia the fruits of all those incalculable benefits which modern science confers (actually or potentially) upon the world. No longer can they insist that Asians should at the same time adopt conceptions of thought and life which are alien to the styles of their own great civilizations. Meanwhile the newly awakening peoples of Africa should have full opportunity to borrow from non-European sources in their social and national development. Europeans must follow the lead of doctors like Albert Schweitzer, of teaching engineers like Rewi Alley, surgeons like Norman Bethune, sociologists like Verrier Elwin. They must cease to appear to the great majority of humanity in the guise of the inventors of the 'know-how' of napalm, of saturation bombing, of the atomic bomb itself.

Science is something which can only be shared in fullest freedom among all the world's peoples. Most of these, indeed, and not only Europeans, cut and laid its very foundation-stones. And each people should freely develop the intrinsic consequences of their own centuries of thought, being in no way bound to adopt the thought-forms which developed in Europe; still less their current vulgarizations. European culture should take its place in an equal brotherhood of cultures; 'neither afore nor after other; without any difference or inequality'.

It is not to be denied that Europeans are called upon to make a certain moral effort in accepting this view of the situation. It is common to hear Westerners say that Asia has merely copied the intellectual and technical achievements of Europe. Europeans, it is implied, bore the burden and heat of the day in forging the instruments of all the modern sciences, and now Asians enter into the enjoyment of the hard ground-work previously done. But this historical perspective is wrong in many ways. To learn to use modern techniques is never mere copying, because it implies that people learn to understand their theory, and since the knowledge of nature is never static and never complete, many inevitably go on to extend its frontiers. Moreover, to suppose that pure and applied science sprang fully formed from the body of the European Renaissance is entirely false; there had been a long preparation of centuries which had seen the absorption by all Europe of Arabic learning, Indian thought, and Chinese technology.

The physico-mathematical hypotheses of Galileo can hardly be visualized without Indian numeral notation. The arsenal in which he set the scene of one of his world-changing dialogues could not have accomplished much without mastery of the characteristic Chinese technique of iron-casting. And again, the early phases of science in Europe were not so laborious and difficult as some would like to think; on the contrary, there were periods when great discoveries could be made at every scratch of a scalpel – once the basic technique of discovery had been discovered. It is impossible as well as absurd, therefore, for Europeans to think of science as their private property. It is not something which they can use to impose their own traditions and way of life on the rest of the world. It is not something for which they can take out an everlasting patent.[1] Always it has belonged to the world community.

---

[1] At one point during the Persian oil dispute of 1951, my eye was caught by a headline in one of the British newspapers which referred to the 'Oil Grab Men'. On looking more closely, I found, to my surprise, that the persons in question were not the foreigners who had until then been in control of Persian oil, but the Persian prime minister, Dr Mossadeq, and his colleagues who were nationalizing it. Such a reversal of the terms which might otherwise have seemed appropriate was at first startling. But I reflected that the apologists for foreign exploitation of the oil would undoubtedly argue that if it had not been for occidental technology and occidental enterprise the oil would in all probability have been lying unused in the earth's bosom still. No doubt this is historically true, but what non-Europeans will never admit is that Europeans were and are justified by their high technical level in exploiting the natural resources of other people's countries for their own advantage.

The Dialogue of East and West

IGNORANCE AND HISTORY

Since pride is often accompanied by ignorance it is not surprising to find that even well-educated Europeans generally show gross lack of knowledge, and even lack of interest, in the history and thought of the Asian peoples. Chinese, Indian, and Arabic studies are even now the Cinderellas of Western European universities, and often treated, if and when pursued, as the investigation of dead things irrelevant to the modern world. British speakers have been heard to maintain that since we alone understand true democracy it is our duty to impose our conceptions even by force upon the non-European inhabitants at least of colonial territories – yet they admitted, upon being asked, that they had never heard of the *panchayat*, or the *asabiyah* of Ibn Khaldun; of Mencian authority for tyrannicide, the civil service examinations of the Thang dynasty, or the Yü Shih Pu (the 'Censorate').[1] In ignorance of the most elementary facts of Chinese, Indian, or Arab history, Europeans or Americans within the framework of the United Nations (so lamentably situated) think nothing of trying to impose their own concepts, the fruit of absolutely different historical developments, upon the representatives of countries which seem (to the unseeing eye) miserable and inferior because as yet they lack the full force of modern industrial power.

Take again the question of languages. One of the worst features

---

[1] The *panchayat* was of course the council of five elders spontaneously elected by the ancient and medieval Indian village. The *asabiyah* was the mystical sense of brotherhood and vocation, which, according to Ibn Khaldun (fourteenth century), the father of social history, inspired the early Islamic states. Mêng Tzu (Mencius), in the fourth century B.C., distinguished between assassination of a tyrant, which might be a righteous deed, and regicide, the wicked murder of a good prince. It is now generally admitted that the civil service examination system, which in China goes back to the first century B.C., was in fact the model for the examinations introduced in Europe and America after the French Revolution. The Yü Shih Pu was a Chinese governmental organization which despatched 'Censors' throughout the country, having independent authority as imperial representatives to report on the justness and uprightness of provincial administrators. That they often did so at the peril of their lives was the theme of much literature and drama. See p. 113 below.

of the situation in Malaya was that for the past half-century only the smallest minority of civil servants saw fit to learn any Chinese. How many French officials in Indo-China really knew the languages of those countries? How many Arabists were there among them in North Africa? Few foreign businessmen in the Chinese treaty-ports before the war ever bothered to acquire the Chinese language sufficiently to entertain a conversation with an educated group. Recently the editor of a famous scientific abstract journal in England, though desirous of receiving current Chinese periodicals, declined to have the papers in them abstracted unless they were already summarized in English, French, or German. And this although Chinese has long been an official language of the United Nations.

The same applies to the world's literatures. A non-European, unable to read any European language, who should stand in the great dome of the British Museum reading-room, and wonder what all this vast mass of books really amounted to, would be thought a laughable barbarian. Yet there are other literatures of comparable scope, the Chinese for example, of which most Europeans can decipher not one word. They themselves are in this respect barbarians. It is true that there have been notable translations of the Chinese classics and of Chinese poetry, but in extent and variety of genre and subject-matter they are still totally insufficient.

Occidental ignorance extends not only to political and philosophical history but also to the history of science and technology. Most people regard this as a highly academic subject. Yet if science has been the true unifier of our world, its history acquires unexpected importance. For example, a writer in *The Times*, no less than the Keeper of the Oriental Books and MSS. in the British Museum itself, stated in 1952, with regard to the Tunhuang MSS., that while block-printing was known and used in eighth-century China, it was left to Europeans to devise printing with movable types. This is of course nonsense; the second invention is due to Pi Shêng (*fl. c.* A.D. 1060), who used porcelain or earthenware, while the Koreans were doing a good deal of printing with copper or bronze founts at the end of the fourteenth century, i.e. well before the time of Gutenberg. Yet the Museum of Printing at Mainz contains no reference to the Chinese inventions, and organizers of commemorative exhibitions in our own country have generally been loth to acknowledge them.

It is often not realized that European superiority in technique is a very recent phenomenon. Marco Polo (about A.D. 1280) found Hangchow a paradise compared with anything that he knew in Europe. As late as 1675 the Russian Tsar asked for the services of a group of Chinese bridge engineers. As late as the early nineteenth century the Chinese wanted practically nothing of what Europe produced, and Europe was sending missions of investigation down to the middle of the century to search out the secrets of traditional Chinese industries (ceramics, textiles, dyeing, tea, lacquer, etc.).

Much depends, for our world outlook, upon the estimate which we place upon the rise of modern science and technology in Renaissance Europe. If Galileo and Vesalius, Newton and Leibniz, Vieta and Harvey, were essentially a racial, a genetic, phenomenon, then we are the people and wisdom was born with us. But perhaps second thoughts would suggest that the structure of European society might have had something to do with the matter. It certainly differed deeply from the bureaucratic feudalism of Asia. If other civilizations perhaps lacked the social conditions which proved the essential fostering soil of this plant, must we now refuse to share its fruits with them? Pushing even further back, perhaps differing social conditions may have owed something to different geographical environments. In any case, nothing suggests that the men and women of the other civilizations do not make as good scientists and engineers as anyone born in Europe.

That the Greeks owed an incalculable debt to the Babylonians and ancient Egyptians is now generally accepted. But there is also a mass of evidence not as yet fully appreciated by Europeans, which shows that during the first fourteen centuries of the Christian era, Europe accepted from Asia a host of fundamental inventions and discoveries, often not knowing very clearly where they had come from. In the time of Robert of Chester and Adelard of Bath

Europeans had to learn Arabic in order to acquire the best that was to be had in science and learning, and from the Arabs and the steppe peoples they received not a few techniques which took their places in the foundations on which the Renaissance built. How many people realize that the system of star co-ordinates universally used by astronomers today is essentially Chinese and not Greek? How many people appreciate that the technique of those deep bore-holes which bring to the modern world the universal fuel, petroleum, can demonstrably be traced back to the engineers of ancient China? Europe boasts of the exploratory voyages of Columbus and other navigators. Europe does not so readily inquire into the inventions which made them possible – the magnetic compass and the sternpost rudder from China, the multiple masts from India and Indonesia, the mizen lateen sail from the mariners of Islam.[1]

But it will be said that the foundations of science were laid by the ancient Greeks.[2] These estimable people (though they produced many men incontestably great) are still receiving more than their fair share of credit. According to a recent formulation, it was the Greeks who first attempted to determine the conditions requisite for the establishment of general truth, and to distinguish science from opinion. Yet this entirely overlooks the work of the Mohists, and the Confucian doctrine of the rectification of names. The Greeks, it is said, were the first to think about the respective

[1] Europeans generally speak as if the whole world had been discovered by Europe. This is a very limited conception, not true at all before the Renaissance. The Greeks in Bactria did not discover China; on the contrary, it was the Chinese (in the person of Chang Chhien) who discovered them. No Roman, so far as we know, ever got as far east as would have corresponded to the coming of Kan Ying and other Chinese to the Persian Gulf. By the middle of the Ming dynasty the Chinese flag was seen all over the Pacific from Zanzibar through Borneo to Kamchatka.

[2] Most biologists talk as if Europeans had been the only people ever to *classify* fauna and flora, for example. But Europeans must cease to be indifferent to the achievements of other peoples. Over the centuries the Chinese developed immense systems of classification of plants, animals, and diseases; not of course with the systematic accuracy of a post-Renaisasnce Linnaean world, but very remarkable nevertheless. In certain respects, indeed, the ideographic language was particularly favourable for this work, as was appreciated in fourteenth-century Persia.

contribution to knowledge of experience and reason. Yet this was precisely the substance of the argument between the Taoists and the Naturalists.

ABSTRACTION AND LAW

That the Greeks were the first to conceive of the Euclidean ideal of a body of natural knowledge logically deduced from a limited number of axioms may indeed be granted. But has this devotion to the abstract always been a beneficient ideal in Europe? Roman law, though a great intellectual achievement, could lead to paradoxical injustices impossible in Chinese jurisprudence.[1] Medieval scholastic philosophy, spinning its webs between the stems of uncriticized premises, turned before long into the abominable dogmatism of the Inquisition.[2] Many Western economists in the nineteenth century encouraged the idea of labouring men as so many 'hands', and of the national homes of colonial peoples as just so much 'territory'. Though modern statisticians have achieved much of value, flesh-and-blood individuals tend to vanish in their world, and it is characteristic of the condition of the

[1] It is of much significance that (as Hudson and Boxer have pointed out) nearly all the early Portuguese travellers in China in the sixteenth century, who had ample opportunity of seeing the working of the law from beneath, reported in glowing terms upon the care which was taken by the Chinese magistrates to see that justice was done. The Portuguese were not surprised at the medieval barbarities of the prisons, which were about on a par with those of Europe, but they were convinced of the superiority of Chinese juristic methods and found that life was counted less cheap than it was in their experience of the West. In this they confirmed earlier impressions of which they never knew, notably that of a Timurid embassy of the fifteenth century.

[2] It is relevant and significant that Chinese history contains nothing really comparable with the European Inquisition. There is doubt about the historicity of the 'Burning of the Books' by the first emperor Chhin Shih Huang Ti, and although in later ages there were many attacks on the Buddhists, in which thousands of monks and nuns were secularized, they were not put to death for their religion. Of course there was political persecution through the ages as now one party was dominant, now another, and the so-called 'literary inquisition' in the Chhing dynasty, directed to rooting out books written by supporters of the Ming, was of this kind; it was an inquisition without *autos-da-fé*. India too showed through the centuries remarkable examples of religious toleration.

European mind that religion should be the only means of bringing them back again. Whatever may be said of Asian failure to develop modern natural science,[1] it does not seem that Chinese or Arabic social philosophy, at any rate, ever lost sight of the concreteness of humanity.[2] The world of today would do well to approach Asian humanism in a more receptive spirit.

Constantly it is said that man's (i.e. Western man's) overwhelming control of natural processes in the atomic age has outstripped his own moral strength and psychological development. Before it is too late, let him take one at least of the essential steps towards self-knowledge, that is to say, knowledge of others. Let him study the words of their saints and sages as well as those of his own. Let him experience his own humanity in the image of theirs.

An outstanding instance of European spiritual pride concerns law and jurisprudence. The highly abstract character of Roman law (so congruent with Euclidean geometry) has been praised for centuries. The Code of Justinian is rightly regarded as a great monument of European culture, and Anglo-Saxons are proud of their structure of case-law and precedent accumulated over the centuries. But in self-satisfied aloofness, European jurists have produced few scholars who were prepared to study the achievements of other peoples in this important field. Early British administration in India did, it is true, lead to a certain interest in Indian customary law, but it was neither sympathetic nor long-lived. The name of but one scholar in all Europe today is renowned

[1] In spite of the start of several centuries which Europe has had in science and technology, many world views are still to be found there which are more parochial and more backward than some which were produced in Asia long before the era of modern science.

[2] My aim is not to idealize Asian social philosophy, but to redress the balance. Asia has suffered just as terribly as other parts of the world from wars, social oppression, and natural calamities such as floods and droughts. The lot of the masses of the people varied greatly; in China, for instance, it was much better during stable dynasties than at times of dynastic collapse. Certain problems, such as the control of the great rivers, were probably formally insoluble until the coming of modern technology, though the history of hydraulic engineering in China is long and heroic.

for his work on Chinese law. Yet the Chinese had had an immense and remarkable legal tradition, and it was based on principles quite different from those which prevailed in Europe. While the West has a penchant for legal fictions, Asians are less deceived by professional sophistry.[1] There was throughout Chinese history a resistance to codification, a determination to judge every case on its own merits, a passion for compromise and harmony. There was hardly any rift which put society asunder which Chinese juris-consults could not join together. Ancient and medieval China knew the rule of law, but consciously preferred the rule of equity.

Then in our own time came the League of Nations, followed by the United Nations. Agreements among sovereign states dedicated to the Rule of Law. But whose law? European law, of course; who could take seriously any other? No voice of dissent, of course, from internationally prominent Asian lawyers all trained at occidental universities; and therefore knowing little or nothing about the history of law in their own countries. Indeed, one of the evil influences of the West (seen in countries like the Philippines) is the emergence of a group of lawyer-politicians. Then comes crisis, and the interpretation of terms such as 'collective security' by the best (Western) legal minds.[2] The Western attitude is that one should always take advantage of a point if the letter of the law is on one's side. One should act 'according to the rules of the game' assuming that in course of time one's adversaries would take advantage of an equal number of like opportunities. Thus the principle of 'collective security' having been erected into a logical and abstract theoretical structure, one should go ahead and apply

[1] Historians, looking back upon our own times, will probably select as an example of a legal fiction outstanding in scope and ramifying results the inter-pretation by the UN-controlling powers of 'China' as meaning a small minority of refugees from that country.

[2] C. P. Fitzgerald, in his excellent *Revolution in China* (Cresset, London, 1952), has given three outstanding examples of Western legalistic thinking which China could not appreciate. First, the shooting down of students demonstrating in Shanghai (May 1925) against arrest of strikers in a Japanese mill, (pp. 53 ff.). Second, the arguments (1927–37) concerning the status of the international settlements (p. 203). Third, the 1945 American airlift of Kuomintang troops to North China and Manchuria, though these areas were effectively communist-controlled (p. 86).

it no matter what the concrete circumstances might be. But Asian systems of jurisprudence have not been so prepared to sacrifice the spirit to the letter.

Of course, law has always had the function of 'acting as a brake upon inevitable social change' (Eggleston). Chinese jurists were often no less reactionary than those of the Temple in London whose papers the rebels went first to burn upon reaching the capital in A.D. 1381. But the genius of a people may moderate even social factors which are similar everywhere, and Europeans should cease to think that they have nothing to learn from the legal systems of Asia.

DEMOCRACY AND BUREAUCRACY

The Occident is torn today between rival conceptions of democracy. Christian conviction and centuries of theology (an inheritance which the Eastern European countries share equally with the Western) have induced a profound belief in the value of the individual, and his or her right, from childhood upwards, to the fullest possible development of innate capacities. But the conception of democracy varies enormously in different parts of the Occident. Most Englishmen cannot conceive of any system of democracy other than that of parliamentary representation, with its special virtues such as the security of the person. An American cannot think any system democratic which does not hold before each log-cabin child the prize of White-House achievement. The Russians cannot imagine any truly democratic system without free educational opportunities for every individual, and the guarantee of full employment. The Yugoslavs value participation in day-to-day industrial administration.

Perhaps the oppositions of some of these points of view would seem less irreconcilable if anyone ever looked outside Europe and asked whether China, India, and Arabia had anything to teach on these subjects. Reference has already been made to some of their contributions. Was not the *carrière ouverte aux talents* a Chinese invention made nearly two thousand years before Europe heard of it? Did not the 'divine right of kings' persist in Europe for at least a similar length of time after the rulers of China had accepted the theory of the Mandate of Heaven? And as to Heaven was it not said, 'Heaven hears as the people hear, Heaven sees as the people see'? And were not those rulers admonished to 'love what the people love, and hate what the people hate'? Was spontaneous local government unknown in ancient India? Who put brotherly love and respect more firmly into practice (irrespective of colour) than the followers of the Commander of the Faithful? Who stated the principle of the 'right of rebellion against unchristian princes' twenty centuries before Bishop Ponnet? [1]

Particularly relevant to our present anxieties is the Chinese experience of bureaucratism. The humanization of bureaucracy is probably the greatest problem of modern civilization, and it presents itself as absolutely vital on both sides in the 'cold war'. A high degree of bureaucratic government seems quite inevitable given the technological complexities of modern society, but modern science has provided a thousand aids and adjuncts which could make it work well. These are as yet very imperfectly used. Telephones, portable radio communications, automatic card-filing and sorting systems, calculating machines, photographic documentary reproduction – all these and many more are available. Nothing is lacking except goodwill. Goodwill is the commitment to treating ordinary people with sympathy and understanding, and the realization that no expenditure on equipment is wasted which sets forward this aim. This is the promised peace on earth, and whoever puts first the real needs of real people will inherit it. Let us hope that the bureaucracies of the future will function with as much true humanism as a good *hsien*-city government under the dynasties of Thang or Sung. That was the time when poets like Su Tung-Pho and Pai Chü-I, scholars like Shen Kua, were officials. If this was not changing philosophers into kings, it was certainly making poets bureaucrats, and if we for our part had given a man

---

[1] A sixteenth-century English churchman who stated with particular clarity this old patristic doctrine in the interests of Protestantism. One of the first things the Parliament did during the Civil War was to reprint him.

such as William Blake such a charge, we might face the Asian tradition with a better countenance. Here the Chinese may have a great task to perform in the teaching of the rest of the world, for their bureaucracy has an experience of two millennia. There may yet be virtue in Confucian traditions, as there was in the eighteenth century when the Latin translations of the classics revealed to an astonished world the existence of a morality without supernaturalism, and of a great continuing culture which had emphatically not been based upon the pessimistic doctrine of original sin.

Many other aspects of this problem might stand out in a Confucian light. Looming upon the world is a great unanswered question: what is science really for? If the Western world has thrown religious sanctions out of the window, can we afford to kick even ethics downstairs? Perhaps the whole world as well as China needs Confucius, Mo Ti, and Lao Tzu more desperately than ever.

UNITY AND CONTRADICTION

Many Western Europeans and Americans feel themselves the representatives of a civilization with a mission to unify the world. The civilization of the Occident alone, they think, is universal. This is because it is itself united, itself a unity, itself the One capable of subsuming all the others, the Many. Such pretensions are baseless.

From the beginning of their thought-history, Europeans have passed continually from one extreme world-outlook to another, rarely finding any synthesis. On the one hand there was God, or the gods, with accompanying supernatural assemblies of angels, spirits, demiurges, entelechies, and the like; on the other there were atoms and the void. Theological spiritualism and mechanical materialism maintained perpetual war. The former component arose, no doubt, from Israel and the ancient civilizations of Egypt and Babylonia, the latter was mostly a product of bold Greek thought. Not until the time of Leibniz and after were any serious attempts made to reconcile this divergence, and no great success was attained until our own time.

It ought therefore to be more widely recognized that Chinese civilization never participated in this disjunction of thought. Organic naturalism was the *philosophia perennis* of China. Fundamentally neither the Confucians nor the Taoists had any use for the supernatural whatever its form – but the mechanical interplay of atoms was not appreciated either. Though atomic theories were always being introduced from India and elsewhere, they never gained any permanent acceptance. When Chinese thought found its greatest expression in the Neo-Confucianism of the twelfth century A.D., it appeared in a shape remarkably akin to the general world-outlook of modern science. Nothing more was necessary for the construction of the universe than matter-energy on the one hand, and organization (at numerous levels of complexity) on the other. The single act of creation was not felt to be a necessary notion. Nor is it possible to accept the contention that Europe has been the centre from which radiated the idea of making the human race one single society. 'Within the four seas all men are brothers' is a Confucian statement belonging to the fifth century B.C. and never subsequently forgotten. In India, Kabir was only one of many poets and prophets of human solidarity. Even in its most enlightened moments, Europe is liable to make unwarranted pretensions.

Europeans, therefore, should devote much greater attention than they have so far been willing to do to the philosophies of Asia. And they should so devote it with intellectual humility, not the closed mind of *a priori* superiority. Much may be learnt which will moderate the common Western European belief that not only science and technology, but also philosophical truth, must necessarily radiate from that peninsular continent to illumine the heathen.

We have noted the historical fact that modern science and technology grew up in Europe and its extension in the Americas. Everyone in these countries accepts this fact as a matter of course. It is probably the main half-conscious self-justification for those feelings of superiority which many of them still entertain towards other peoples. How little real ground there is for this attitude has already been indicated. But what is often not so clearly recognized is that the psychology of dominance which has for some centuries past characterized the peoples dwelling round the Atlantic seaboard has been the direct result of that vast power over nature which the scientific movement of the Renaissance brought forth. Today this psychology has become a menace to the world.

Naturally it began in a small way, and of course with war techniques. Chinese and Arab fire-lances and barrel-guns of primitive kinds (tenth to thirteenth centuries) were quickly developed in fourteenth-century Europe to form the artillery which battered down feudal castles and, in the seventeenth and eighteenth centuries, the forts of Indian princes. Cortes had armour, weapons, and horses which in the sixteenth century overcame without much difficulty the obsidian clubs of Aztecs and Mayas. The boisterous merchant captains disliked by coastal Chinese mandarins in the seventeenth century reappeared before long in the guise of nineteenth-century admirals of the fleet to force opium through the inadequate defences of Commissioner Lin Tsê-Hsü. In the later nineteenth century the pace quickened in all continents. And now no longer is there talk of annexation or 'protection', for empire-building has gone out of fashion. It looks much better, no doubt, to have small sovereign states sitting in the United Nations, with strings which can be pulled from behind the scenes. This in itself might be considered a concession to modern sensibilities. But we still face the imposition of characteristically West European ideas upon other peoples under threat of destruction by the most up-to-date weapons; with Korea as the object-lesson of what will remain of a country after it has been 'liberated' by modern means. Truly there is no solution save an understanding of the worth of the cultures of other peoples, and a realization that the West European or American 'way of life' cannot and must not be forced upon them.

TOWARDS WORLD COMMONWEALTH

Knowledge of Nature is no one's private property. The world is like a holy vessel, says the *Tao Tê Ching*. Whoever grabs at it will lose it irretrievably. How can anyone hope to keep secret for ever the information that precisely two milligrams of vitamin B_1 are necessary each day for the health of one human individual? The impact of modern Western civilization on China and other Asian countries has inevitably induced in their people a determination that they too must share in the higher standards of life which modern science and technology have placed at the disposal of modern man. They insist upon moving forward to a point at which all can satisfy what we now know to be the minimal needs of civilized human beings. And in some cases they have decided (as in China) that they would do this by a mighty leap, short-circuiting long periods comparable with those of the 'dark Satanic mills' of nineteenth-century Europe, the miseries of the 'Industrial Revolution'. This whole movement is one of primary historical significance, and the more Occidental peoples oppose it, the worse will the judgment of world history be on them. How then should Europeans and Americans react to these events? By a policy which denies United Nations representation to six hundred million people? By maintaining pirate strongholds off the China coast? By prohibiting the export of sulpha-drugs and antibiotics which the Asian masses so greatly need? Somehow or other the West must understand that to the average Asian man or woman the whole current mobilization of the self-styled 'free world' seems directed, not so much towards the 'containment of communism' as against the rising upsurge of political consciousness, the national independence movements, and the struggle for industrialization and the raising of living standards of all Asian and African peoples.

Perhaps the whole question reduces to the active practice of humility and brotherly love. We need a real conviction that all racialism, all self-satisfied beliefs of cultural superiority, are a denial of the world community. We need a list of diabolical clichés, for example, that Asian people 'cannot be understood'. We need to free ourselves from what Claude Roy has so well called 'the iron curtain of false enigmas'. Europe and America must stand ready not only to share with all Asians and Africans those treasures of understanding and use of Nature which modern science and technology have brought forth, but also to learn from them many things concerning individual life and society which they are more than competent to teach. If this is not done, the achievements of Europe (and America) will in any case become the common property of mankind, but our civilization will go down to history as distorted and evil, unwilling to practise what it preached, and worthy of the condemnation of ten thousand generations.

2

THE PAST IN CHINA'S PRESENT

First published in *The Centennial Review*,
4, (Nos. 2 and 3) 1960.

INTRODUCTION

The ensuing notes are based on discussions of the Oxford Political Study Group at Nuffield College and of the Universities and Left Review Club in London early in 1959. A biochemist by profession, I do not regard myself as primarily a student of contemporary affairs, nor am I a political economist, still less a journalist; but in the course of work with a number of collaborators on the history of science, scientific thought, and technology in the Chinese culture-area,[1] I have found myself deeply concerned with the origins and development of that culture, and have come to see its current changes against the social and philosophical background of many centuries. Indeed, I believe that only so can they be properly understood and appreciated by people of other cultures.

In the adoption of communism by China, this social system and philosophy has for the first time entered (in the language of physical science) a new and different 'phase', has diffused across the boundary between two of the great historical civilizations, has been transplanted from one of these vast social organisms to another. Everything has to be learned about this great pheno-

---

[1] J. Needham, with the collaboration of Wang Ling (Wang Ching-Ning), Lu Gwei-Djen, Ho Ping-Yü, Kenneth Robinson, Tshao Thien-Chhin and others: *Science and Civilisation in China* (seven volumes in twelve parts) (Cambridge, 1954-); hereinafter abbreviated as *SCC*.

menon. To what extent did Chinese culture contain a *praeparatio evangelica*? How will it mould the gospel of collectivism in the future? Did China perhaps send contributions westward in earlier times from which it germinated? Such are some of the questions which surge into the mind.

BUREAUCRATIC FEUDALISM: THE NON-HEREDITARY ÉLITE IN THE NON-COMPETITIVE SOCIETY

Let us begin with a brief discussion of China's social structure through the ages. It is probably impossible to understand contemporary China without realizing that great modifications of social class-structure are involved there. If one does not feel sympathy with the urge towards a unitary class-structure of society, the desire for a socialist order, there is little hope of understanding what the Chinese are trying to do. On the other hand, it is quite clear that throughout history the class-structure in China was not at all identical with that of the West, though similarities were by no means absent.

It must at once be said that when one enters into the question of Chinese social structure, one finds oneself in the presence of a great debate which is as yet far from being concluded or even brought to a focus.[1] Although there are many differences of interpretation among scholars, I feel quite satisfied on the broad principle that during the past 2,000 years, roughly speaking, China did not have feudalism in the aristocratic military Western sense. Whether the Chinese system is known, as it was by the founding fathers of Marxism, as the 'asiatic form of production', or as other people have called it, 'asiatic bureaucratism' or 'feudal bureaucratism', or as the Chinese very often call it, 'bureaucratic feudalism', or whatever other term one likes to adopt – it was certainly something different from anything that Europe ever knew. Sometimes I

[1] See the judicious essay of D. Bodde, 'Feudalism in China', in R. Coulborn, ed., *Feudalism in History* (Princeton, 1956). p. 49; as also, of course, the classical writings of H. Maspero, 'Le Régime Féodal', etc., in *Mélanges Posthumes sur les Religions et l'Histoire de la Chine*, Volume 3 (Paris, 1950); and M. Granet, *La Féodalité Chinoise* (Oslo, 1952).

have been tempted to regard it as a disappearance of all intermediate feudal lords at an early stage in the unification of the
empire (after the time of Chhin Shih Huang Ti in the third century
B.C.), and the rule of the country by only one feudal lord, namely,
the emperor, operating and exploiting by means of a hyper-
trophied instrument, the non-hereditary civil service, the bureaucracy, the mandarinate, recruited from the 'scholar-gentry'. It is
debatable to what extent this should be called a 'class' because it
is clear that in different times and to different degrees it had a great
deal of fluidity. Families rose into the 'estate', if you like, of the
scholar-gentry and sank out of it again; and during those periods
when the imperial examinations played an important part in the
recruiting of the civil service, families which could not produce
the right talents and the particular skills and gifts for success in the
examinations and the bureaucracy, were not going to survive
more than a generation or two at a high level of society.

Thus the *shih*, the scholar-bureaucrats, were the literary and
managerial élite of the nation for two millennia. We must not
forget, therefore, that the conception of the *carrière ouverte aux
talents* was a Chinese invention and not a French or a European
one. Indeed, it has been shown by chapter and verse that the
theory of competitive examination for the civil service was taken
over by the Western nations in the nineteenth century in full
consciousness of the Chinese example,[1] even though the sino-
philism of the Chinoiserie period had long given place to a certain
disillusionment regarding the Celestial Empire and its mandarinate
as a College of All Sages. Of course, the mandarinate was not as
'classless' as has sometimes been made out, for even in the best and
most open periods, boys from learned homes which had good
private libraries had a great advantage. But in any case, the scale
of values of the scholarly administrator differed profoundly in all
ages from that of the acquisitive merchant.

Here there is no space to go into the details of this non-
hereditary civil service which became so supreme in Chinese

[1] Têng Ssu-Yü, 'Chinese Influence on the Western Examination System,'
Harvard Journ. Asiat. Studies, **7**, 267 (1943).

society after the Chhin and Han, but immediately the fundamental
fact of its existence is stated, one can see its relevance to what is
happening at the present time.[1] Surely the basic conception of a
non-hereditary élite in a non-competitive society has much in
common with the conception of membership of an organization
like the Party, especially when linked with the keen social morality
now renewed in China. Is there not something strikingly similar in
the dissociation of prestige and leadership from birth and wealth?
Moreover, today we no longer have civil servants or bureaucrats
of the old style entirely devoted to *theoria* and knowing nothing of
praxis, but, on the contrary, an élite which understands a great deal
about *praxis*, has itself participated in productive work, and may
be doing so at the same time as fulfilling its administrative func-
tions and in accordance with the new moral emphases. In other
words, a communist ethical and sociological dynamic has built
upon age-old Confucian instinct in forming the basic inspiration
of the officials and peoples' leaders of today and tomorrow.

THE INHIBITION OF THE INDIGENOUS DEVELOPMENT OF CAPITALISM

The bureaucratic-feudal system of traditional China proved to be
one of the most stable forms of social order ever developed. From
the time of the first Chhin emperor in the third century B.C. down
to that improbable medical revolutionary of 1911, it played a
leading part in assuring for Chinese culture a continuity shared
only partially by Israel among all other nations of the world. But
above all it meant (as in India) that there was no indigenous development of capitalism.[2] The mandarinate system was so
successful that it inhibited the rise of the merchants to power in
the State; it walled up their guilds in the restricted role of friendly

[1] A lapidary description of the essentials of traditional Chinese bureaucratic
society and their significance for modern developments has been given by
E. Balazs in *Asiatische Studien*, 1953, 77.

[2] As Schurmann has shown, in discussing traditional Chinese property concepts
in *Far Eastern Quarterly*, **15**, 507 (1956), the basic idea of individual *freies eigentum*
on which capitalist society was built was absent in China.

and benefit societies; it nipped capitalist accumulation in the bud; it was always ready to tax mining enterprises out of existence and to crush (as it did in the fifteenth century A.D. after the death of Chêng Ho)[1] all mariners' efforts towards sea trade and expansion; and finally, most significantly, it creamed off for two thousand years the best brains from all levels of society into its own service. This last function alone might temptingly offer itself as an aid to explaining why the feudal system could have given way to capitalism in the West as it did, while bureaucratic feudalism continued calmly on its way. The hereditary aristocratic principle was not calculated to get the best brains into the positions of most power, and when the brightest minds found themselves in merchant business or as royal advisers rather than short-circuited in the hierarchy of the Church, the days of Western feudalism were numbered. In China, on the other hand, the fact that the administrators were drawn from the most intelligent men of their age meant that they did not arouse among the population that intense dissatisfaction with effete and inefficient descendants of aristocratic houses which must have played a great part in the downfall of Western feudalism.

It is necessary therefore for Westerners to realize today that for the Chinese, capitalism was something essentially and intrinsically foreign, something imposed upon them at a certain time by Westerners enjoying a military strength based for a few short centuries on their fortuitous development of modern technology. Nor did capitalism in China follow quickly upon the first contacts with Westerners. The Portuguese merchants of the sixteenth century and the Jesuit missionaries of the seventeenth had no effect whatever upon the nature of the Chinese economy, great though their influence was in other ways. Not until the beginning of the nineteenth century, at the time of the Opium Wars, was it borne in upon the scholar-gentry that modern industrialization was really inevitable. Hence there supervened an interesting transition period

---

[1] The famous eunuch admiral. For his voyages, see J. J. L. Duyvendak in Yusuf Kemal, *Monumenta Cartographica*, Vol. 4 (1939), pp. 1411 ff., and *China's Discovery of Africa*, (London, 1949). See also *SCC*, Vol. 4, Pt. 3, pp. 486 ff.

when some of the leading bureaucratic officials such as Tsêng Kuo-Fan, Tso Tsung-Thang, and Li Hung-Chang set up arsenals and factories with funds part-private and part-bureaucratic, and with engineers from abroad.[1] This type of industry, however, naturally lacked the long organizational experience possessed by Western firms, and proved unable to compete with them, so for most of the century Chinese governments and officials found it easier to grant concessions and let the foreigners do the work which they understood. The resulting stranglehold greatly discouraged Chinese-owned enterprise, and it was not until the First World War, when the European powers temporarily relaxed their profit-making activities in China, that indigenous Chinese capitalist industry got a chance to develop. This was based on a new group of people, so small in number that it is difficult to call it a class, which had long been associated in a comprador capacity with the enterprises of foreign firms in China, and which had been successful in applying modern banking methods to Chinese conditions. Even so, it never conquered sectors wider than those of light industry, most of the mining and heavy industry remaining in the grip of foreign interests together with most of the railway transport. Still, it was in strong alliance with them against any socialist movements, and naturally tended to make itself respectable by associating with the most highly respected scholarly official families. The Kuomintang party was nothing but the outward expression of this inward social reality, and its organs of repression had to be quite sharp because in the last analysis capitalism was a form of society which the Chinese had never been accustomed to, did not want, and were less and less prepared to accept. The permanent nightmare of the Kuomintang was that the 'dark Satanic mills' of uninhibited capitalist enterprise were evidently

[1] See the three books by Chhen Chhi-Thien, *Lin Tsê-Hsü, Pioneer Promoter of the Adoption of Western Means of Maritime Defence in China* (Peiping, 1934), *Tsêng Kuo-Fan, Pioneer Promoter of the Steamship in China* (Peiping, 1935), and *Tso Tsung-Thang, Pioneer Promoter of the Modern Dockyard and the Woollen Mill in China* (Peiping, 1938). Compendious and relatively new is Têng Ssu-Yü & J. K. Fairbank, *China's Response to the West; a Documentary Survey* (Harvard, 1954).

not the only gateway to modernization and industrialization.[1]
Another and a better road lay open.

THE NEED FOR QUANTITATIVE ACCOUNTING

One of the most important aspects of the classical mandarinate was
what I call its 'nosphomeric' character. Probably the reader has
never encountered this word before, but that would not surprise
me because I invented it myself. It takes me back to a place in
Kweichow province during the war where the Bishop of Hongkong and I both had to 'anchor' (as the drivers' fraternity used to
say) because our trucks were out of order. Thus we had to stop a
few days at the little mountain town of Annan. We talked a great
deal about the question of 'graft and squeeze'. 'Old China Hands',
of course, would descant for hours about the practice of graft and
squeeze at all levels in traditional Chinese society, and I came
across it myself in many cases. For example, I met one old *hsien
chang* (city magistrate) in Kansu province, an aged man who used
to tell how things were done in the old days – how when the
chuang yuan in charge of eight counties came round, there would
be a supper with chopsticks and bowls all of silver, and these
would be sent round to his apartment afterwards. This had been
done for centuries; it was the recognized thing. It was his 'rake-
off', and everything went well as long as people did not take more
than their proper rake-off and did not upset the system by trying
to be 'honest' and refusing these things. It was part of the way the
society worked. The old expression, *ta kuan fa tshai*, 'to rise in the

---

[1] The resolve to move directly from traditional Chinese society to socialism
was extremely clear and explicit in the writings of the early Chinese revolutionaries
of the anti-Manchu period. They were also highly conscious of many precursor
features in traditional Chinese thought and life which were congruent with
socialism; indeed, they touched in one place or another upon most of the matters
which are discussed in the present review. See a recent interesting analysis of the
writings of such men as Fêng Tzu-Yu, Chu Chih-Hsin, and Liang Chhi-Chhao
about 1906, by R. A. Scalapino & H. Schriffrin in *Journ. Asian Studies*, **18**, 321
(1959). The book by J. R. Levenson, *Liang Chhi-Chhao and the Mind of Modern
China* (Harvard, 1953), is also worth reading, though marred by a slant of
ironical disparagement of the great struggling intellectual figures with whom he
deals.

civil service and acquire great wealth', was the standard thing in classical Chinese society, and it is clear that this ought not to be called 'graft and squeeze' because it was the way in which a non-currency society operated. Since from ancient times the taxes were collected at the periphery and sent to the capital in the form of actual kind, of barges loaded with rice or other grain, or bales of silk, and since also it was the practice in most dynasties never to pay a living wage to provincial officials, it was obvious that the only thing that they could possibly do to run the local show was to take their ten per cent or whatever it was, and this was accordingly done. I therefore said to Bishop Ronald Hall, 'What we want is a non-pejorative word for graft and squeeze'. After he left next day at about five o'clock in the morning, I found when I got up a little piece of paper under my door saying 'Acts 5:1'. When I got to a Bible and looked this up, I found it was the story of Ananias and Sapphira who kept back part of some money which was supposed to be given to the church. Although St. Peter disapproved of this, with serious consequences to the poor bene-factors, the word used in the text has itself no bad connotation. So, as *nosphizein*, meaning to sequestrate, and *meros*, a part, gave just the word wanted, I therefore invented and still propose to use the term 'nosphomeric hydraulic (see p. 42) Asian bureau-cracy'.

What has all this to do with the issue? Just that profound changes in administrative 'morality' had to accompany social and industrial changes if the old society was to be transformed into a modern nation. I knew personally many men in China during the war who did not care to make the old society work, who felt that it was totally out of keeping with modern needs, who were, in fact, believers in what one might call 'quantitative accounting', and not prepared, for example, to sign as having received ten dynamos when in fact they had only received eight. I knew engineers who lost their jobs and had plenty of trouble with the Kuomintang in consequence. These men were good engineers, knowing little about communism and often quite non-political. They were really the forerunners of what we must call the new

moral emphasis. This is a cardinally important feature of communist China and derives directly from the creation of a new
society. It is not unlike the new ethos of business morality which
grew up in the early period of capitalism when there was a similar
association between puritan morals and quantitative accounting.
But the parallel is at a different level; in China the new élite are
not building upon the old basis. In fact, they have arisen because
they alone are appropriate to a socialist society based on natural
science and technology. This can only work by quantitative
measurement and impersonal, though not consequently inhuman,
computation; and the new moral emphasis, deeply Confucian, as
we shall later see, is the characteristic ethical accompaniment or
superstructure of a society which may well continue to be
'hydraulic' but which in a neotechnic age can never again be
'nosphomeric'.

CIVIL VERSUS MILITARY ETHOS

Another very vital aspect of the bureaucratic form of feudalism
was that it generated a civil and not a military ethos in Chinese
society. I remember once, about 1943, sitting in a very dirty little
village street at the time of a truck breakdown with Sir Frederick
Eggleston, who was then Australian Minister in Chungking. We
were putting in time while waiting by drinking tea in one of those
chha kuan or teahouses in the street of a Szechuan village. Seeing
before our eyes the general medieval conditions, the lack of
sanitation, the poverty of the people (all very different from what
one finds in villages now), he turned to me and said, 'Why, at any
moment one might imagine a knight and a troop of men-at-arms
come riding down the village street'. To which I replied, 'Well,
yes and no, because in fact it would have been a rather cultured
person in a litter, certainly not wearing armour. The men-at-arms
would have been very poorly equipped, and, in fact, the magistrate would have been ruling basically by the prestige of literary
culture, enormously important in Chinese traditional society, and
not by open dominance and force'.

I did not mean, of course, that the ultimate sanction was not force, as in all societies which man has known. But one can hardly over-estimate the significance of the radical absence of the aristocratic principle in traditional Chinese society through the ages. Broadly speaking, the aristocracy, such as it was, comprised merely the relatives of the reigning imperial house, and its members, kept rigidly under control and not allowed to enter the bureaucracy, were always under suspicion as possible contending figure-heads, and went altogether into oblivion when the dynasty changed. The last thing they were allowed was military command. It is a commonplace to refer to the old Chinese proverb about not using good iron to make nails and not expecting good men to become soldiers, but I believe that it represents something permanent in the Chinese scale of values. Here, of course, there is a tremendous contrast with Japan, where the feudal values were much more similar to those of military medieval Europe. It is true that China today takes great (and, indeed, legitimate) pride in the feats which were accomplished in the Korean war, when the Chinese army stood up to the best-equipped Western troops which could be brought against them in a way that had not hitherto been known in the last three or four centuries of history. It was a very different story, indeed, from the Taku Forts, for instance, or anything that happened in the Opium Wars. Nevertheless, I consider that this classical predominance of the civil as against the military ethos will continue to give to Chinese society a basically pacific outlook for many centuries to come.

ORGANIC UNITY OF RULERS AND PEOPLE

Certain traits in Chinese society are very persistent. Here I am not thinking of the quotations from the Confucian or Taoist classics, which many Chinese Marxist leaders often include in their writings, but all along the line one sees an emphasis on unification of and with the people. This is not a new thing; it existed in all the best ages in China. 'Heaven sees as the people see; Heaven hears as the people hear.'

For example, when I was in Peking in the summer of 1958, there was great enthusiasm about the dam which was being built in rapid time, largely by the voluntary labour of the citizens of the capital, to make a lake which would be valuable for the irrigation of the dry and dusty plain north of the city, and in which the Ming tombs would be mirrored. It was notable that Mao Tsê-Tung himself and the members of the Central Committee went out, and like most other people in Peking, did their day or two shovelling earth and doing other construction jobs. This was the symbolic blessing for a widespread movement during the past two years when great numbers of administrators have returned for a time to the farm and the bench to renew their experience of how it feels to be one of the working people. Indeed, I should not hesitate to regard these manifestations as the extended modern equivalents and lineal descendants of the ancient rite in which it was customary for each emperor and his ministers to plough the ceremonial furrows every year. One of the great annual cere-monies in the old days, this solemnity, carried out at the Temple of Agriculture in the south of the city, symbolized the organic unity of the Son of Heaven and his people before the powers of Nature. But in socialist China, the distinction between rulers and ruled has disappeared. 'Every cook must learn to rule the State', and every administrator must remind himself periodically of how it feels to be cook and carpenter. The principle of unity which the sages and good officials of old understood is thus manifested as never before.

The converse of the respect entertained by the emperor for the people was the very deeply based respect for authority which throughout the ages was felt by them. The emperor was the Son of Heaven. He had a mandate from Heaven to rule 'all under Heaven' (i.e., all China); but this was something very unlike the 'divine right' of kings in Europe. The emperor's right was con-ditional. In ancient times he was held responsible in person for the prosperity of the country, in particular for securing the right sort of weather for agriculture. As high priest of a cosmic *numen* as well as king, he offered sacrifices on behalf of the whole people, securing the blessing of Heaven not only by them but also by himself behaving in the way which Heaven approved. By Heaven's mandate he ruled as long as his rule was good – but if it degenerated, natural calamities such as flood and drought would come as warnings, and rebels would arise to claim the mandate. If there emerged a successful pretender to the throne, or a new and more powerful dynasty, it was always held that the previous imperial house had forfeited the mandate from Heaven by not behaving in the way appropriate to imperial rule. Thus the dual function of priest and king evoked in the Chinese people a very deeply based respect for authority. It generated the idea that a government is not simply a thing which has been created by a man, not something which has come about because one man is more powerful than another, but that it is part of a certain cosmic order. Such conceptions are surely close to modern Western thought about social evolution, trends of history, and revolutionary necessity based on concrete social forces.

THE HYDRAULIC TRADITION AND PUBLIC WORKS

There is another important feature in the social background of present-day China. One of the best-known theories about the origin of bureaucratic feudalism in China maintains that it was connected with the overwhelming importance of hydraulic engineering in ancient times. I believe there is a great deal in this opinion (though some of the loudest proponents of it can be remarkably tedious), and I found when I was in China during the war that a great many Chinese historians think so, too. The reason for the necessity of irrigation goes back to the geographical and indeed the geotectonic character of the country. The importance of irrigation canals for intensive agriculture, water conservancy for preventing floods, and canal transport for the gathering in of the tribute to the Imperial Court from the provinces, led to the establishment of a veritable tradition of great public works which is absolutely living in China today as much as it ever was in the Han or the Chhin or the Thang dynasties.

All this illustrates and symbolizes the tradition of great public works which exists in China and which is still in full vigour. In fact, the role of the Party there, in putting the accent on great public works, is something which is much less new to Chinese society than it might be to any other nation in the world, except, perhaps, the Egyptians and the Sinhalese. Here, again, contemporary China is very much in line with the best and most brilliant dynastic periods of traditional China.

THE TRADITION OF NATIONALIZED PRODUCTION

Westerners should remember, moreover, that in China there is a very old tradition not only of great public works, but also of 'nationalized production'. People who are not familiar with Chinese history, or not very familiar with it, perhaps do not realize how ancient this is. It goes back at least to the fourth century B.C., possibly to the fifth century B.C. in proposal form, but it was actually enacted in 120 B.C., just before the time when the Old Silk Road began to carry caravans of Chinese produce, especially silk, to Persia and the West. Then, when we come to 81 B.C., we get that truly marvellous work, the *Yen Thieh Lun* (Discussions on Salt and Iron), still well worth reading today by anyone interested in economic history,[1] which purports to be a verbatim account (it is not really so, of course, but it is not far off) of a great debate held about 83 B.C. between bureaucratic officials and feudal-minded Confucian scholars who were not convinced of the necessity for a powerful civil service. The point at issue was, of course, the 'nationalization' of salt and iron. I am quite aware that the word 'nationalization' must not be used with regard to these things with exactly the same meaning which we apply in speaking of nationalization in the modern sense. Yet it was definitely a take-over of the production of salt and iron by the State, and officials were put in charge of it. A number of Iron

[1] A partial translation by E. M. Gale, *Discourses on Salt and Iron, a Debate on State Control of Commerce and Industry in Ancient China* (Leiden, 1931), exists, continued by E. M. Gale, P. A. Boodberg, & T. C. Lin in *Journ. Roy. Asiat. Soc. (North China Branch)*, **65**, 73 (1934).

Bureaux were set up all over the country where iron was smelted and cast. Iron casting was already a well advanced technique in second-century B.C. China, though not mastered until the fourteenth century A.D. in any other part of the world,[1] and the function of the Bureaux was to make cast-iron agricultural tools, such as hoes, spades, and ploughshares. At a later period in the Han there were further measures of nationalization, bringing under government control the making of wine and beer.

Thus national ownership of the means of production is something clearly in the traditional background of modern Chinese thinking, and although I have given Han examples, it is possible to get many others from later periods (for example, the Sung) in the Middle Ages. Such conceptions of State control, therefore, are not for the Chinese daringly revolutionary, but rather a natural development arising out of their own history. Here is a very vital point in which Chinese attitudes differ from those of some Western peoples who have been so permeated by the conceptions of individual capitalist industrial enterprise during the past three hundred years.

It is not that enterprise is lacking. Much in China today reminds one of the parallel of the American frontier in the nineteenth century, the expanding opportunities of the Far West. This is now being repeated with all its implications for the development of the Central Asian parts of China, yet under the inspiration of socialist co-operative altruism, not of individual aggrandisement or money-making.

THE ORDER OF PRECEDENCE OF THE ESTATES

In connection with this question of State production, I should like to refer next to the traditional order of precedence of the estates of Chinese society. We need not call them classes; indeed, it may

[1] See *SCC*, Vol. 5, Part 1, and, in the meantime, J. Needham, *The Development of Iron and Steel Technology in China*, the Dickinson Memorial Lecture (London, 1958); or, more shortly, 'Remarques relatives à l'Histoire de la Sidérurgie Chinoise' (with English translation) in 'Actes du Colloque International "Le Fer à travers les Ages",' Nancy, 1955, *Annales de l'Est*, No. 16 (1956).

be very dangerous to do so without further thought. Most people probably know that famous phrase, *shih nung kung shang*, the four estates of society: the scholars, then the farmers, then the artisans, and finally the lowest 'class' of all, the merchants. Assuredly this is one of those patterns which are always at the background of the Chinese mind.

This traditional proverbial phrase has been resounding down through the centuries ever since the end of the feudal period and the beginning of the unified Empire in the third century B.C. The low emphasis placed on merchants as well as the parallel low emphasis placed on soldiers is, I think, quite significant for the instinctive mental attitude of the Chinese people at the present time. The ruin of Kuomintang China was quite naturally attributed to the nefarious activities of the banker-comprador-merchant group, and according to my experience, intellectual and university circles during the war were never in any way enamoured of the unclassical Kuomintang, with only very few exceptions. They were not at first sympathetic to the Communists either (I shall have more to say about that presently), but they certainly had no conviction that Kuomintang capitalism represented the natural line of evolution of Chinese culture. Perhaps it was the instinctive knowledge of the Kuomintang leaders that their economic system was profoundly un-Chinese which led them to talk so much about the feudal virtues, and to try to popularize forms of social asceticism such as the New Life Movement which assorted very oddly with the accumulation of great wealth in few hands. The paradoxical result could not avoid a strong impression of hypocrisy, and in fact only a very small percentage of the intellectuals were attracted by it.

The Kuomintang order was implicitly *shang shih kung nung*, and everyone could see that it was un-Chinese. The orthodox communist order was obviously *kung nung shih shang*, and the Party under Mao Tsê-Tung saw at an early stage that this could not work either. The solution was found first in *nung kung shih shang* for immediate results, and in the total scrapping of all such distinctions for the long-term programme.

THE MYSTIQUE OF FARMING

Now, with the position of farming[1] we come to another point which illuminates, I think, more of the background of current thought in China. Farming was always recognized as fundamentally important; the farmers were anciently high up in the scale. They were the second in honour, ranking immediately after the scholars. Chinese culture has always embodied a deep love of the countryside, which, after all, did occupy ninety per cent of the people. A certain moral stature of the farming people, or the peasant farmers, if you like, is very marked in Chinese culture. Just as in Roman times there was a great *mystique* about the return of the senator or the consul to his birthplace, the return to the farm, the return to the soil, to till the fields again which his ancestors had tilled, so also this pattern is very much present in Chinese feeling, even in aesthetic appreciation. The theme of the *Kuei Thien Lu*, constantly recurring, is an example of it. So many poets wrote of a return to the country, a homecoming to the ancestral farm, a getting away from public life, a resigning of official appointments, the hanging up of official hats, and the retirement to the countryside.[2] This is a very great feature of typical aesthetics throughout the ages. One must understand that the Communist Party in China derived a great deal of moral stature from the very fact that it had lived 'in the wilderness' (though this is not quite the right term, but in the country) with the peasants. In other words, it has had the attributes of a 'country party' (though in a very different sense from the party of the same name in Australia). To be revolutionary and rural at one and the same time

---

[1] The classical book on Chinese agriculture in English is that of F. H. King, *Farmers of Forty Centuries* (London, 1927), but it should now be complemented by the admirable study of R. Dumont, *Révolution dans la Campagne Chinoise* (Paris, 1957).

[2] See, for example, the famous essay of Thao Yuan-Ming (A.D. 365–427) translated by H. A. Giles in his *Gems of Chinese Literature: Prose*, 2nd edition (Shanghai, 1923), p. 103. Cf. also his translation of Liu Yü-Hsi's (A.D. 772–842) essay on the same theme, p. 148.

was a feat which could have succeeded only in China perhaps, and yet one which was essential for gaining and keeping the leadership there.

THE MYSTIQUE OF MANUAL WORK

Closely allied to the classical admiration for farming there went throughout Chinese history an appreciation of the dignity of manual work. It may not have been the dominant tradition among the literati, but it was emphasized century after century by the poets. No doubt this is one reason why Tu Fu, Pai Chü-I, and other great classical poets are so appreciated in contemporary China, for time after time they praised the farmer, satirized the bureaucrat, and castigated the callous military officer. Perhaps this tendency was partly connected with the paramount necessity for some at least of the officials to have a good knowledge of water conservation, public works engineering, transportation techniques, and military technology. Abundant instances could be given, but it may suffice to mention a few outstanding names such as Chhao Tsho and Chang Jung in the Han, Yuwên Khai in the Sui, and Su Sung and Shen Kua in the Sung. Typical reforms periodically introduced, such as those of Wang An-Shih in the eleventh century A.D., made medicine, botany, geography, and hydraulic engineering parts of the imperial examination system. When Yen Yuan, an eminent scholar of the early Chhing period who had himself studied and practised medicine, undertook in A.D. 1694 to establish a new type of education, he laid much emphasis on practical and technological subjects. The Chang Nan Shu Yuan, as it was called, had not only a gymnasium but also halls filled with machines for demonstration and practice, special rooms for mathematics and geography, and facilities for learning hydraulic engineering, architecture, agriculture, military arts, applied chemistry, and even pyrotechnics. But, of course, the contrary attitude of aloofness from manual and practical work was also very common in China, where the culture of the administrators was, after all, primarily literary.

All cultures and civilizations have suffered from the divorce of *theoria* and *praxis*. But the greatest thinkers, experimenters, and artists have always seen that only when the manual and the mental (or the intellectual) are combined in one individual's experience can mankind reach its highest stature. This combination has been of the greatest importance in the history both of theoretical science and of technology; it gave weight to the materialist speculations of the pre-Socratics, it brought out the best in Aristotle, and it inspired the Renaissance engineers whose genius culminated in Leonardo. Men like Palissy, Perrault, Newcomen, Watt, Stephenson, and Edison fill the subsequent centuries. Moreover, the combination not only brings true knowledge of Nature, but also deeper sympathy with those members of society whose contribution must still for some time to come be primarily manual.

There is no question that at the present time a great *mystique* of manual work has grown up in China. I believe that this is a true expression of the mass feeling of the people, guided, perhaps, by the party leadership, but by no means something imposed from above. It was inevitable and necessary that it should happen some time if the Chinese people were to coalesce into a single, unified and as far as possible classless society. There may be exaggerations in particular times and places due to excessive enthusiasm, but the movement is fundamentally sound. To think of manual work as a humiliating punishment in China is a lamentable misunderstanding propagated by certain Western writers.

Yet the present valuation of manual work in China, it should be emphasized, is but a passing phase. Such work is not regarded as an ultimate end in itself, but a means of bringing the intellectual and the non-manual workers into more fruitful relation with the material world, and giving them in the process better understanding of their fellow men. On the other hand, the farmers and workers greatly welcome this opportunity of personal contact. Meanwhile, every form of mechanization is being pushed ahead as fast as possible. At the Ming Tombs Reservoir Dam in the summer of 1958 there were bulldozers, graders, and an elaborate earth-fill supply system of railways, both standard gauge and narrow. But the voluntary participation of hundreds of thousands of ordinary citizens of Peking was meant to be a demonstration of their solidarity with the whole working people, as well as an expression of determination to get on with the job of re-creating their vast country. In Szechuan a moving remark was made to me by a Chinese friend who pointed to the children on the pavement watching the hauliers working their great loaded carts up the hills, and said, 'With the truck production rate the way it is now, or better, when those boys grow up they'll never have to do that back-breaking work – it will be altogether a thing of the past!'

MORALITY AND MACHIAVELLIANISM

Before leaving altogether the subject of the civil service, we might consider for a moment what some people call tough-minded realism and others Machiavellianism. A curious paradox occurred recently. A scholar of Columbia University has written an interesting, but in my opinion perverse, book on the history of the bureaucratic-feudal civil service in Asian countries.[1] Intending to delineate the characteristics and origins of hydraulic bureaucratic feudalism in many different parts of the world, he seeks to refer back to it all the most unlovely manifestations of State power and coercion in modern societies. Omitting all reference to such phenomena as city-state tyranny or oligarchic dictatorship, to Byzantine autocracy, absolute monarchy, or imperialism, to the Holy Inquisition, or to the fascist forms of developed capitalism, he fixes (most unjustly) upon Asian bureaucratic feudalism as the completest type of tyranny and upon Chinese 'oriental despotism' as the most perfect example of it. The facts disagree radically with his general view, but no matter. To make the readers' flesh creep, he quoted a good deal from the *Arthaśastra*, that great Indian work of the second century A.D. on Machiavellian power-politics. It was quite striking that although his chief fire was directed against the Chinese mandarinate, he was not able to find for his purpose any

[1] K. A. Wittfogel, *Oriental Despotism* (New Haven, 1957).

parallel to this work in Chinese literature. And, indeed, there is no parallel to it.[1]

What the full explanation of this may be is uncertain – perhaps the analogous texts of the Warring States period have not come down to us – but it is certainly true that Confucian sentiment would always have been very much against any such codification of amoral power techniques as one finds in the *Arthaśastra*, with its plain-spoken and even enthusiastic advocacy of the poisoning and torture of opponents, or the use of spies, saboteurs, ambushes, and all kinds of stratagems.

This raises the question of how much hypocrisy there was in Chinese history. No doubt a good deal, as in the history of all nations, but perhaps less than one would think because throughout the ages the best of the scholars were deeply and honestly attached to the high morality of Confucianism. Certainly all the poets emphasized it, and in China many of the greatest poets were officials themselves. After all, there were standard techniques for managing people, if one might so put it, such as gifts of various kinds, reciprocal obligations, customary honours, and so on. Besides, as has been mentioned already, the art of persuasion was of age-old cultivation in Chinese life. It may be that such characteristics originate from special but fortuitous technological features at early stages when a civilization is crystallizing. The eminent sinologist, H. G. Creel, pointed out long ago[2] that in feudal Chou China the lords were poorly provided with defensive armour while the commoners were familiar with a powerful weapon, the cross-bow, long ere Europe had it. Hence propaganda and

[1] Partial parallels may be found in the Fa Chia literature of the fourth and third centuries B.C. (the School of Legalists, cf. *SCC*, Vol. 2, pp. 204ff.), and the use of spies is recommended in the fourth century B.C. military classic *Sun Tzu Ping Fa* (Master Sun's Art of War), cf. L. Giles' translation (London, 1910), pp. 160ff.; but there is nothing approaching the cold-blooded systematization of the *Arthaśastra*. The handiest translation of the latter is by R. Shamasastry (Mysore, 1929).

[2] H. G. Creel, *La Naissance de la Chine* (Paris, 1937), pp. 344ff. His argument is abundantly supported by ancient Chinese texts, for example, *Analects*, XIII, xxx; *Huai Nan Tzu*, chap. 15, translated by E. Morgan in *Tao the Great Luminant* (Shanghai, 1933), pp. 186, 192ff.

indoctrination were raised to a high level as social techniques, as indeed is abundantly evident from many places in the Chinese classics. Again, as perhaps would be expected in a non-industrialized society, austerity of life was blessed by Confucian ethical authority. Of course, there were many exceptions, rulers who delighted in extreme luxury, etc., but they usually came to a bad end, as the Bureau of Historiography never failed to point out. Broadly speaking, the needs even of the high officials were always comparatively simple. All this throws light on the present situation. The Chinese spirit does not admire unprincipled tactics, dishonest dealing, or personal luxury. Behaviour of a competitive or acquisitive character is not considered worthy of the magnanimous man (*chün tzu*), whose place is with the people, like the leaders of the 'bandits' of Liangshan, leading from within, not from above.

THE MANDARINATE AND PUBLIC OPINION

Sometimes it is said that in medieval China there was no such thing as public opinion. I am well satisfied that this is a wholly mistaken idea. The scholar-gentry, and especially those who were in office in the civil service, in the mandarinate, the *kuan liao* people, were extremely influential, and persuasion was their characteristic method. Sometimes they succeeded in gaining the attention and capturing the good will of an emperor for many years, and in other cases, where for one reason or another the emperor 'got across' his civil service, then there were many things which could not happen because the civil service or mandarinate would not give way. It was immensely tied to age-old custom and there were many things on which it refused to compromise. One might mention in passing the institution of the Censorate, the *yü shih* or Yü Shih Pu, which originally grew up as one of the departments of State, and was in its heyday concerned with the control or verification, to use a French phrase, of the functioning of the civil service at the periphery, in the provinces. Many a tale and many an opera theme in old China concerned the actions of censors in bringing abuses to book at great personal risk, and there are many historical instances of the execution or exile of one remonstrator after another failing to silence the protests of the scholars. Thus the literati in the civil service at any particular time, and especially, of course, those at the capital, did constitute a public opinion of a wide and educated character, and this was generally not at all insensitive to the opinions of the mass of the common people.[1]

SOCIAL COHESION: FAMILY, MERCHANT GUILD, PEASANT COMMUNITY, AND SECRET SOCIETY

I am still not able to leave the sociological field because something must be said about the traditions of social cohesion in China. This is a fundamentally important aspect of life and thought in any culture. The first thing one must mention is the institution of the large family.[2] There is no doubt that although during the last 100 years the really large family has been steadily dying out, yet in ancient and medieval times it was a very important reality. Many things were connected with it – that Confucian tradition, for example, which so much disapproved of jealousy; that profound courtesy which was the ideal aim on all occasions; and the phenomenon of 'face-saving', which sprang from a desire to spare embarrassment to others.[3] All this will be rather obvious, I think, to anyone who has read any Chinese literature. The cohesion of a large family depended on forbearance. One of the emperors enquired of an old gentleman who was brought to him as having attained the great aim of the large family, 'five generations in one hall', how it was done and how his family has been so successful. He said, 'It was just forbearance.' The emperor asked again and said, 'It must be something more than that.' But the aged man wouldn't add anything more except that it was all a matter of

[1] See, for example, C. P. Fitzgerald's study of the bureaucracy under the Thang empress Wu Hou, *The Empress Wu* (London, 1956); or J. T. C. Liu, 'An Early Sung Reformer: Fan Chung-Yen', in J. K. Fairbank, ed., *Chinese Thought and Institutions* (Chicago, 1957), p. 105.

[2] Cf., for example, Hsü Lang-Kuang in *Amer. Journ. Sociol.*, **48**, 555 (1943).

[3] Cf., for example, Hu Hsien-Chin in *Amer. Anthropologist*, **46**, 45 (1944).

forbearance, one for the other. I often have occasion to quote from an old man who wrote a book about Hangchow in A.D. 1235. He never signed his name to it but called himself the *Kuan pu nai tê ong:* 'the old gentleman of the irrigated garden who attained (peace) through forbearance'.

In 1958 I travelled some 12,000 miles within the country, by road and plane as well as by train, gathering further material for our work on the history of science and technology in the Chinese culture-area, and meeting hundreds not only of scientists and scholars, but of all sorts and conditions of men. My most outstanding impression was the unreality of the idea so cherished in the West that the population is dragooned to perform its tasks. On the contrary, everywhere one saw co-operation, spontaneity (sometimes outrunning government planning), enthusiasm for increasing production and modernization, pride in an ancient culture equipping itself to take its rightful place in the modern world. What has been done in public health, social services, industrial development, and advancing amenities of all kinds, and what one sees going on under one's eyes, would be absolutely impossible without the willing and convinced co-operation and social cohesion of all age-groups and all types of workers, manual and intellectual. A new type of social engineering, the product of leadership from within, not from above, raises up movements as urgent popular demands and not as any mechanical result of drives from the central government.

The carry-over of the large-family ethos into spontaneous working groups was also observable during the formation of the Chinese Industrial Co-operatives during the Second World War.[1]

[1] An interesting account of years of work with the Chinese Industrial Co-operatives is given by P. Townsend in his *China Phoenix* (London, 1956). Precious reminiscences by one who was described as their 'founder, spark-plug and main-stay', Rewi Alley, are contained in his books *Yo Banfa* (Shanghai, 1952 and Peking, 1955), and *The People have Strength* (Peking, 1954), and are represented also in his poems, collected, for example, in *Gung Ho* (Christchurch, N. Z., 1948). Experiences as a Co-operative Organizer in a very remote part of China are related by P. Goullart in *Forgotten Kingdom* (London, 1955). The magnificent work of the C.I.C. technical training colleges was described in *Training Rural Leaders: the Shantan Bailie School, Kansu Province, China,* published by the F.A.O. (Washing-

It happened that I was closely acquainted with much of that work. During the great *diaspora* when the Chinese were leaving the coastal districts to the tender mercies of the Japanese and were coming over in millions to the western provinces, one found a flotsam and jetsam of artisans from all over the country meeting together and almost spontaneously setting up production co-operatives – paper-makers, shoemakers, foundry workers, and so on. I knew them in many cities, but particularly at Paochi in Shensi. There you could not help feeling that the large-family mentality was at work; they formed rather tight groups which co-operated effectively and ran their businesses often under very considerable difficulties, even in the face of opposition by the Kuomintang government in the later phases of the war.

When we come to the relationship of merchants to one another, it is generally known that China did have merchant 'guilds'.[1] But the merchant guilds in China never acquired anything like the importance in society of the merchant guilds in the West, never became powerful in State government, never encroached, one might say, upon the power of the imperial bureaucratic administration. The mandarinate saw to it that they did not, and as will later be suggested, we have here a good clue to the failure of late Chinese society to generate any Renaissance, and ultimately of its failure to originate *modern* science. In fact, we do not find any conception of the city-state in China. The old expressions *Stadtluft macht frei* (The very air of a city makes a man free from feudal service) or *bürgerliche Rechtsicherheit* (Security of city folk under the law) are meaningless where China is concerned. The city in China was always essentially a node in

---

ton, D. C., 1949). Today these colleges are incorporated in a nation-wide system inspired by the same ideas of public service and retaining much of the original method, while the general conception of rural industrialization on a co-operative basis has become an accepted and integral part of the whole vast re-organization of Chinese society into rational units which combine agricultural with industrial activities.

[1] The standard reference is H. B. Morse, *The Guilds of China, with an Account of the Guild Merchant or Co-Hong of Canton*, 2nd edition (Shanghai, 1932), but the subject needs fuller study.

the administrative network of the Empire, and the whole conception of 'aldermen' or 'masters of guilds' running the city in
an independent way, often in the teeth of opposition from local
feudal lords, and often allied to the royal power – all that kind of
thing was unheard-of and unknown in China. Sir John Pratt made
an interesting and amusing contribution when in one of his books
he recalled how in 1862 some of the Western European businessmen established in Shanghai, one of the treaty ports, petitioned
the Government in Peking for a grant of a city charter.[1] The
perplexity which this caused at the imperial court in Peking must
have been extraordinary, because no one there would have had
the faintest idea as to what they wanted, or had ever heard of such
a thing being granted to any body of merchants. But all this does
not alter the fact that mutual aid occurred in plenty. The Chinese
merchant guilds certainly engaged vigorously in helping their
members. At Chhang-ting in Fukien I once had the pleasure of
staying in one of the beautiful old-style hostel buildings with
courtyards and elegantly carved halls and pavilions which were
put up in different cities for the reception of merchants from other
provinces when they came there to buy and sell. We thus have
another aspect of social cohesion in the merchant guilds even
though they never became important politically, as in Europe.

Another aspect of Chinese life which should not be under-
estimated is the great extent to which mutual aid took place
among the peasant farmers. Throughout the ages there was
co-operation at the village level, sometimes more, no doubt, and
sometimes less.[2] Mutual aid teams were not something absolutely
new and unheard-of when they were encouraged at the beginning
of the present government. In medieval times the affairs of the
village were largely left alone by the administrative officials of the
county town; as long as the *hsiang chang* came up with the right

[1] J. T. Pratt, *The Expansion of Europe into the Far East* (London, 1947), p. 17.
[2] Cf. Tsu Yu-Yüeh, 'The Spirit of Chinese Philanthropy: a Study in Mutual
Aid', *Columbia University Studies in History, Economics and Public Law*, 1912,
No. 125 (Vol. 50, No. 1); and more recently, Yang Lien-Shêng on reciprocity,
'The Concept of *Pao* as a Basis for Social Relations in China', in J. K. Fairbank,
ed., *Chinese Thought and Institutions* (Chicago, 1957), p. 291.

amount of taxes and fulfilled the demands of the corvée or military conscription service, he was free to consult with the clan elders on all matters of land utilization, road and bridge repairs, and other communal questions. I am not trying to idealize the picture or to minimize the extent of thoroughly bad government, rapacious landlords, and rich peasants at different times in Chinese history – only to emphasize that in the better times, at least, mutual aid in the community was a firm reality.

Apart from all this we must not forget to take into account quite another side of the medal – that is, the high degree of cohesion within voluntary and what indeed may be called subversive organizations. Apart from the committees of village and clan elders in different times and places, apart from the old open Taoist or Buddhist societies which engaged in compassionate enterprises like bridge-building and road construction, there were also throughout Chinese history the secret societies.

The importance of these can hardly be over-estimated, for a powerful degree of social cohesion was characteristic of them. Even in our own time no foreigner could live long in China without coming in contact with these societies.[1] Although I personally had no intimate knowledge of them, anyone could sense the strength of the bonds which they could imply, as in the

[1] There is no adequate and systematic treatment of the subject of Chinese secret societies, but one may mention W. Stanton's *The Triad Society or Heaven-and-Earth Association* (Hongkong, 1900); J. S. M. Ward & W. G. Stirling, *The Hung Society*, three volumes (London, 1925); B. Favre, *Les Sociétés Sécrètes en Chine* (Paris, 1933); C. Glick & Hung Shêng-Hua, *Swords of Silence* (New York, 1947); L. Comber, *Secret Societies in Malaya* (New York, 1958); and the extraordinary compilation of M. L. Wynne, *Triad and Tabut* (Singapore, 1941). The Western literature on Chinese secret societies has a peculiar character in which everything is seen as through a glass darkly. This is not surprising, since it constitutes a kind of nightmare folklorism largely based on the depositions of illiterate Chinese working-men to sinologically incompetent police officials. The few books written by capable sinologists have all long been out-dated by the progress of knowledge in Asian studies, but they are still worth reading. I refer to G. Schlegel's *Thian Ti Hwui: the Hung League or Heaven-and-Earth League* (Batavia, 1866), photolitho reproduction (Singapore, 1956); J. J. M. de Groot, *Het Kongsiwezen van Borneo* ('s-Gravenhage, 1885). P. Pelliot's devastating review of Ward & Stirling remains true, alas, to this day (*T'oung Pao*, **25**, 444, 1928).

White Lotus Sect, the Szechuanese *Ko Lao Hui*, or the Triad Society. Even during the Second World War there were secret associations of truck drivers like the *Hung Pang* and the *Chhing Pang*, believed to have descended from pilots' associations on the Grand Canal, and all of us who had to do with trucks came into contact with them. I am not saying that all this was a very desirable phenomenon. Everyone knows that overseas in Southeast Asia these secret societies, which readily succumb to pure gangsterism, have been the cause of a great deal of trouble, and there is little to be said for them. But in traditional Chinese society, in the set-up which we have already discussed – an apparent autocracy but, in fact, a government by custom and compromise, where the Confucian tradition kept things sweet up to a certain point, but where things were liable to go wrong when exceptionally greedy officials arose or when there was a general decay of society, as happened periodically towards the end of dynasties – there one can see the importance of the people's cohesion in the secret societies. Undoubtedly they played an extremely important part in Chinese life.

They were, indeed, closely associated with that great series of popular rebellions which runs throughout Chinese history.[1] Generally these movements arose in their might at the end of effete or tyrannical dynasties; such was the uprising of Huang Chao against the Thang (A.D. 874–84) on the one hand, or that of Chhen Shêng (209 B.C.) against the Chhin on the other. In such circumstances the reigning house with all its hangers-on was usually overthrown, and replaced by a new one emanating from some suitable personality on the rebel side, a new house destined no doubt to accomplish in due course a similar cycle but endowed with a century or two of fresh vigour and good government. Thus the founder of the Han, Liu Pang, was one of the leaders of the revolt against the Chhin, and Chu Yuan-Chang,

---

[1] All histories of China deal with these, whether as large as Cordier's or as concise as Goodrich's. But the special attention given to them is one of the interesting features of *An Outline History of China* (Peking, 1958). A brief treatment worth reading is that of H. Franke, *Geschichte in Wissenschaft und Unterricht*, **1**, 31 (1951), part of his inaugural lecture at Cologne.

1,500 years later the founder of the Ming, had long been in revolt against the Mongol dynasty of the Yuan. Sometimes, however, a great rebellion would occur 'prematurely' and succeed only in weakening the dynasty so that it fell not long afterwards – such was the situation with the Taoist Yellow Turban Rebellion of A.D. 184 and the semi-Christian Thai-Phing Revolution (A.D. 1851–64). This last 'State within a State' was perhaps the greatest revolutionary commonwealth in Chinese history, and is regarded with much pride by contemporary Chinese scholarship, which has devoted deep study to its analysis. Today its banners hang, as if in a Westminster Abbey, in the Great Hall above the Wu Mên gate of the Imperial Palace at Peking.

The bitterness of these class struggles was very great, and a landlord general such as Wu San-Kuei in A.D. 1640 could prefer to join with the Manchu foreigners rather than sink his differences with the successful peasant leader Li Tzu-Chêng. Modern Chinese historians are giving particular attention to the study of these rebellions and to the secret societies, often Taoist or Buddhist in affiliation (since Confucianism was so closely associated with the scholar-gentry), which organized and inspired them. It is as if a revolutionary Germany should trace with loving admiration the exploits of the Anabaptists, or a progressive England commemorate the places where the Levellers and the Diggers performed their historic actions. But while in Europe many of these movements could flourish openly, Chinese society was generally so unified that the oppressed groups had to have recourse to secrecy, establishing an underground resistance pattern which transmitted century after century a tradition of social solidarity.

The lesson for us in all this is that the many examples of extreme individualism among Chinese scholars and thinkers, upon which Western sinologists have so delighted to expatiate, have given a certain distortion to our conception of the Chinese people. The much-advertised eccentric solitaries have, I think, blinded us somewhat to the more essential and deep-rooted cohesive factors in Chinese society. What this clearly leads up to is the cohesiveness of the present time. It forms the indispensable historical background for the mutual aid groups in villages which led on to those co-operative forms of agriculture covering already a couple of years ago ninety per cent of the country, and to the large-scale communes which originated during the latter part of 1958. Rural communist China was not created in a day. The problem was how to capture those Artesian depths of social solidarity emotion which had been one of the main motivating forces of Chinese society for two millennia. No mere nationalism could ever have done this – only a doctrine which could fully evoke that mixture of enlightened self-interest and concern for the happiness of one's neighbour which had welded together the 'black-haired people' indissolubly in a hundred battles against the feudal bureaucrats. The co-operatives and communes are only extensions, I believe, of certain cohesive features in Chinese society which have been developing all through the ages.

As for the new venture of the *jen min kung shê* (translated rather riskily as 'communes'),[1] this development was only just starting when I was last in China, but I conceive it to be primarily an extension of the system of co-operative production which could be seen at work everywhere there. Deeply in accord with old Chinese social traditions, this principle is, I believe, welcomed and accepted by the overwhelming majority of Chinese working people. Current criticism of the 'communes' seems to rest, often enough, on limitations of outlook characteristic of highly industrialized Western societies. People there who dislike the idea of families eating in restaurants and canteens know only Western homes provided with gas stoves, electric washing machines, etc. If they had had any experience of the slavery of the Chinese women throughout the ages to the charcoal or brushwood stove and the primitive water supply, they would understand that the co-operative farm or works restaurant and the public baths today seem more like a heaven on earth to millions. Until recently only the very largest cities had piped gas, running water, and main drainage. Side by side with these improvements an immense effort of re-housing is under way. Emancipation of women to follow

[1] Cf. A. L. Strong, *The Rise of the Chinese People's Communes* (Peking, 1959).

careers, whether on the farm, railway, or in the factory, or in intellectual work, is one of the most remarkable features of present-day China, as I know from personal contacts with many friends all over the country. Nor am I particularly shocked by the idea of restaurants where one does not have to pay, having enjoyed many a meal under such conditions in the kibbutzim of Israel as well as in the educational institutions of my own country. This is a matter of pride in China today, not of compulsion or regimentation – the direct reward of the successes of agricultural production.

ELEMENTS OF DEMOCRACY

Lastly, a word or two about 'democracy'. Most Europeans who have lived in China will agree that although the celebrated Greek origins were no part of the Chinese inheritance, there is a vein of instinctive democracy running very deeply through the culture. The almost complete absence of special 'built-in' forms of linguistic address between superiors and inferiors (so sharply contrasting with Japanese), the age-old recognition of intellectual capacity absolutely irrespective of birth, the profound humanism of Confucian ethics, and the classical acknowledgment of the human dignity of the farmer and the artisan, all illumine a living experience of contacts with and among Chinese people. It will not be forgotten, moreover, that the right and duty of 'rebellion against un-Confucian princes' was a leading tenet of the chief school of Chinese social philosophy for nearly two millennia before the parallel doctrine in Europe received the blessing of the Reformers. One may conclude, I think, that although traditional China had no institutions which we could call 'representative' democracy in the Western sense, it was certainly not, as some have thought, a sheer autocracy. It was a highly constitutional empire, if with an unwritten constitution, and governed profoundly by custom. The representative institution as such is new in China, the elections for membership of State assemblies, for governors of cities, or mayors, as they now call them. Yet a very powerful element of democracy was, I am convinced, present in traditional China.

Many Western observers of contemporary China appear to be haunted by an impression of imposed 'uniformity' in current Chinese life. They seem to entertain some nightmare conception of male and female prison-barracks inhabited by robots with identical responses.[1] I believe this to be quite illusory, corresponding to nothing in my experience of Chinese modern working-class housing, or of the working people themselves. What I can see happening is more like this: when people accustomed to eating meat once a year find themselves able to have it once a week, it is not surprising that they all react in the same way. When people who for generations have hauled barrows groaning over mountain ways, or towed junks upstream against the Yangtze's currents, see for the first time engines coming to their rescue, their reactions tend to be uniform. When scientists who formerly had to waste their best years in empty laboratories feel the support of big financial backing and popular encouragement, their new inspiration takes almost identical shape. These are the deepest 'uniformities' that I can see in China today.

At the same time, it is quite true that the Chinese have adopted wholeheartedly a particular political philosophy, and there is undoubtedly a great deal of social influence on individuals to accept it, but there is much latitude in interpretation. The learned and technical journals, for example, are full of lively controversial articles. Wall newspapers give great opportunity for the expression of criticism on the part of the rank and file in every institution. Moreover, extreme care is taken to foster all kinds of new ideas arising among the mass of the people, and to encourage originality.

[1] Here the official Chinese translators of current Chinese Government information services and bulletins have been somewhat at fault. Knowing probably only the American connotation of the word 'dormitory', i.e., a building containing a number of small 'apartments' (or, in British usage, 'flats'), they have succeeded in giving to Europeans the somewhat bizarre impression that large sections of the Chinese working-class had been induced to abandon family life and to sleep in segregated halls holding as many beds as hospital wards or the 'dormitories' of English 'public schools'.

It was very moving to see in Chinese cities in July of 1958 the processions and the rejoicings in honour of local inventors and innovators. *Kan hsiang, kan shuo, kan tso!* (Dare to think, dare to speak, dare to act) was the watchword painted on every city and temple wall in China that summer – this does not seem to me the kind of slogan which one would expect in a dictatorial authoritarianism.

CONFUCIAN MORALITY AND TAOIST SOCIAL PROTEST

Let us now turn to the consideration of certain matters more on the philosophical and ethical plane. Of course, we have already touched upon some aspects of ethics, but we need to put this in its correct perspective by recognizing the existence of an essential wallpaper of the Chinese mind today and for the foreseeable future – the background of Confucianism and Taoism. I say this with the parallel in mind that however revolutionary any European, for example, may be, he will have as the inevitable background to his mind the social righteousness of Israel, the subtleties of Greek philosophy, and the logic of Roman law, three elements all embodied in the Christian Church and the Holy Roman Empire. These fundamental conditioners of thought cannot be deleted from the European past.

We have already said a word or two about the moral austerity of ancient or classical Confucianism, which was essentially a system of ethics and not in any way a metaphysic. The Confucian ideal was a state of social justice in so far as this could be conceived of within the framework of the feudalism of Master Khung's own time (the sixth century B.C.). Its conservatism arose from the fact that the relation of prince and minister or master and servant was included among those five human relationships which Confucius invested with particular sanctity. But the idea that every person exists in a kind of concrete special functional relationship with every other person in society is one which is capable of perpetual renovation; loyalty to your commanders is needed in a Red as well as in any other Army, and filial piety must necessarily appear in new forms when family allowances or full old-age pensions and suitable new State-provided modes of life for the aged come into general acceptance.

Confucianism was a religion, too, if you define that as something which involves the sense of the holy, for a quality of the numinous is very present in Confucian temples (the *wên miao*); but not if you think of religion only as the theology of a transcendent creator–deity. The emphasis of Confucianism, of course, was always on duties rather than rights, and this again is familiar in modern as well as in traditional Chinese society. There has been little change in that respect. In the past Confucianism tended a good deal towards asceticism and even a certain prudery, and these ancient presences can be felt very much among the communists of today and in their social attitudes.

But the Taoists are immortal as well. The ancient Taoist philosophers were men who made a powerful social protest against the feudal society of their time.[1] They refused to co-operate with it. The famous expression *chün hu! mu hu!* of Chuang Chou, for instance, in the fourth century B.C., when he says, 'Princes, indeed! Grooms to be sure!', in other words, those who know only the distinctions between princes and grooms, how you should salute one and how you should salute the other, we spew them out of our mouths. This is not true knowledge. We believe in obtaining a real knowledge of Nature and a real understanding of the ceaselessly changing universe. We retire from human society, we walk outside human society, we resort to the mountains and forests, we contemplate Nature, we cultivate our receptivity, and we teach abstention from all force and coercion. 'Production without possession, action without self-assertion, development without domination.'[2] And there they were in their

[1] For a more detailed account, see *SCC*, Vol. 2, pp. 33ff., and especially pp. 86ff., 100ff.

[2] These words, which must be a translation of the latter half of ch. 2 of the *Tao Tê Ching*, were quoted by Bertrand Russell in *The Problem of China* (London, 1922), p. 194.

hermitages and abbeys all through history, refusing to co-operate in the bureaucratic-feudal society.

That element of Taoist renunciation, and that element of Confucian ascesis, neither of them springing from any supernaturalism but in the interests of high morality, are very powerful indeed at the present time. The vein of puritanism, in fact, in modern China is not at all new. It is something which has been there all through the ages. It has reminded some observers of the Ironside spirit in seventeenth-century revolutionary England, with the age-old humanistic moral conviction of Master Khung taking the place of that of the prophets of Israel's God of righteousness. The reforming of the old decayed society and the assertion of moral values, if no doubt occasionally carried to rather absurd lengths, is thus not a new development, but a restoration of something exceedingly old. In fact, I should go so far as to say that although neither Confucianism nor Taoism, in spite of some appearances, ever involved the conception of a creator or an omnipotent transcendent deity in the usual sense, they were wholly devoted, each in their diametrically opposite way, to bringing about what in early Christian terms would be called the 'Kingdom of God on Earth'.

It has been instructive in recent years to see the reassessment of the ancient philosophers going on. When I was in China in 1952, it was interesting to see that only three individual characters were emphasized in the magnificent teaching exhibition of archaeology and history from the Bronze Age onwards which is established in the Imperial Palace Museum, the Ku Kung Po Wu Kuan at Peking. They were Mo Ti, the fourth century B.C. philosopher of universal love, and Hsimên Pao, the great hydraulic engineer and humanitarian of the sixth century B.C.; this latter official is remembered not only for having built some of the earliest dams and reservoirs, but also, according to a story which is not at all unhistorical, for having ended the sacrifice of girls to the god of the Yellow River, so he was a humanitarian and a hydraulic engineer at the same time. The third hero emphasized was Kungshu Phan, or Lu Pan, the great artisan and patron saint of artisans. But when

I went back six years later, I found that while the three heroes were still there, Confucius, Mencius, and even Hsün Chhing, as well as most of the other classical philosophers, had been added, emphasis being laid on Confucius chiefly as an educator. All of them are now well represented and described with suitable exhibits.

A great debate is always going on, of course, as to how far Confucius himself was a revolutionary. There is no doubt that he was in the field of education, for he did away with the ancient idea that noble birth was an indispensable requirement. He was prepared to educate anyone who was capable of receiving it. This was how he became the patron saint of the bureaucracy, for all the posts needed officials and the Confucian education was the most suitable for them. But the question is more complex than this, for it turns on the extent to which Confucius was consciously opposed to the whole system of bronze-age proto-feudalism, and in favour of more collectivist forms. There is, at any rate, no doubt that some of his recorded actions indicate this, and that some of his descendants played a part in those popular rebellions of which we have already spoken. A strong case for the politically democratic character of Confucius has been made out by the sinologist H. G. Creel in a fascinating, if somewhat controversial, study.[1] Actually, Kuo Mo-Jo himself, the great archaeologist and ancient historian who is now president of the Chinese National Academy of Sciences, has gone on record quite a number of times for what one might call the progressive view of Confucius as opposed to the other view, held of course by many Chinese Marxists, that he was nothing but a reactionary of deepest dye. It was natural that they should think so, for in modern times and under the Kuomintang, many landowners and traditionalists of all sorts upheld Confucianism as one of the conservative institutions they wished to defend.

The reader may complain if no word is said about Buddhism. In my opinion (and again this is a personal one), it never played

---

[1] *Confucius, the Man and the Myth* (New York, 1949; London, 1951).

anything like the same part in China as the two indigenous doctrines. It is very curious that although philosophically 'other-worldly', for economic reasons it came to be allied with peasant struggles, and in some periods at least as much so as the Taoists. But presumably because of its emphasis on compassion, the *karuna* aspect of Buddhism, alongside that of emptiness (*śunya*), it was very important and early in the field with regard to the establishment of hospitals, orphanages, and similar institutions. It has certainly not been without influence on modern reformers and revolutionaries.

NEO-CONFUCIANISM AND DIALECTICAL ORGANICISM

When we pass from the ethical to the metaphysical, a number of points arise which are of as great if not greater importance than anything yet said. The school to which I particularly want to draw attention is the Hsing Li Hsüeh Chia, creators of the great scholastic synthesis of the eleventh and twelfth centuries A.D.[1] The greatest representative of the Neo-Confucian school was Chu Hsi, who was born in A.D. 1131 and lived throughout the rest of the century. The earliest was Chou Tun-I, born in A.D. 1017, and three other great names come in between. It is highly characteristic of their philosophical position that Chu Hsi has been termed both the Herbert Spencer and the Thomas Aquinas of China.

What may have been an important factor in the rallying of the Chinese intellectuals to the communist point of view is the fact that Neo-Confucianism was closely related to dialectical materialism. In other words, this system of thought, which was really the culmination of Chinese philosophical speculation throughout the ages, was a materialism, but it was not a mechanical materialism. It was, in fact, an organic conception of Nature, a theory of

[1] A detailed account is given in *SCC*, Vol. 2, pp. 455 ff. Such recent publications as Chou I-Chhing's *La Philosophie Morale dans le Néo-Confucianisme* (Paris, 1954), and A. C. Graham's *Two Chinese Philosophers* (London, 1958) are well worth study.

integrative levels, an organic naturalism,[1] having nothing to do with an external transcendent creator-deity or supernatural being of any sort, but at the same time leaving all possible room for man's highest experiences, highest indeed of the successive levels of organization and integration in the world of Nature. It was thus essentially not dualistic. It was, if you like, holist. It was therefore closely allied to the conceptions of dialectical materialism, which is also a materialism but not a mechanical one, and pictures a dialectic in Nature such that contradictions are constructively resolved at a series of integrative levels (plant, animal, social, etc.); the series of the *scala naturae*, in fact, with all the transitions between its stages.

The Neo-Confucian school operated with two fundamental conceptions, *chhi* and *li*. *Chhi* originally meant something rather ✓ like the Greek *pneuma*, a vapour, something like a gas or an emanation, but by the Sung it had come to mean all matter, the grossest as well as the most tenuous. As someone recently pointed out very acutely, it is rather remarkable that *pneuma* became more and more rarefied in Europe as the centuries wore on, while *chhi*, on the other hand, became more and more material. This must be connected with the characteristic Chinese love of pragmatic concreteness. As for *li*, the word began by meaning a way of cutting jade according to its natural pattern, and eventually came to mean essentially all structure in Nature itself – 'natural organic pattern'. These words are absolutely not translatable by Aristotelian matter and form; they have at first sight some similarity

[1] Exactly what I mean here has been set forth, with documentation, in earlier publications; see especially my Herbert Spencer Lecture at Oxford University, *Integrative Levels, a Revaluation of the Idea of Progress* (1937), especially page 40; reprinted in *Time, the Refreshing River* (London, 1943), in which see especially pp. 184ff., 233ff. The relevance of organic naturalism (as in Whitehead, Sellars, Smuts, Lloyd-Morgan, etc.) to dialectical materialism, indeed a close logical relationship, may be found further in J. Lindsay, *Marxism and Contemporary Science* (London, 1949), especially pp. 70ff. The most recent world picture in this tradition, drawn, however, neither by a professional philosopher nor by a marxist theoretician, but by a brilliant and unorthodox Jesuit, is *The Phenomenon of Man* by P. Teilhard de Chardin. Fr. Teilhard de Chardin spent many years of his life in China, working in the Chinese Palaeontological Survey.

with those concepts, but at bottom they are not at all similar. Then there are many other important technical terms, like *chhêng*, for example, which some people translate as 'sincerity'. I have a fixed conviction that it ought rather to be rendered the 'precise fulfilment of an organic function', with all that that implies. Among the most profound of Neo-Confucian ideas is that embodied in the famous phrase *wu chi erh thai chi*, 'that which has no Pole and yet itself is the supreme Pole', namely, the conception of the whole universe as an organic unity, in fact, as a single organism.[1]

EUROPEAN SCHIZOPHRENIA AND CHINESE UNITARINESS

In all this one might think that we were getting far away from contemporary China. Not at all. The enthusiastic acceptance of dialectical materialism in China is regarded by many Westerners as a great mystery. They marvel that such a people could have accepted what at first sight might seem so European with alacrity and conviction. Yet I can almost imagine Chinese scholars saying to themselves, 'How astonishing; this is very like our own *philosophia perennis* integrated with modern science and at last come home to us.'

It is important to notice how deeply opposed is this non-dualistic, organic conception of the universe to what I intend in

[1] Certain Neo-Confucian terms and conceptions might still be useful today. As J. Lindsay has pointed out (*loc. cit.*, p. 91), we find it hard to speak of the forms of 'organized-ness', the x-factor at all the successive levels, which makes the difference between random collocations and wholes or entities, at each new level 'making all things new'. 'Vitalist theories like Lloyd-Morgan's', he says, 'or organicist theories like Whitehead's try to fill the gap with spirit, élan, *nisus*, God, or a metaphysical principle of creative purpose. Almost the whole of language is soaked with anthropocentric attitudes. We simply do not possess a word which can simultaneously express the activity of the atom and the activity of the human being. We can express mechanical relations and we can express personal relations; but we lack the integrative vocabulary'. Here *li* is exactly what is wanted – the pattern-principle operating in diverse ways at all levels, but a term without any theological or metaphysical undertones, and not at all anthropomorphic. If clues such as this are followed up, Neo-Thomism may run into serious competition.

due course to call, adopting a phrase from Lancelot L. Whyte,[1] the 'European dissociation'. By this I mean that confused dance in which Europeans have engaged from the earliest times, oscillating between theological spiritualism on the one hand and mechanical materialism on the other. What difficulty the Western world had in attaining equilibrium! On one side there was the tradition of atomism starting with Democritus, Epicurus, and Lucretius, and continued by atheist science all down the ages. On the other there was the tradition, emanating perhaps from Israel rather than from Greece, which laid emphasis on the spiritual reality of the Creator and the angelic host, upheld by priests and prophets. This dualism mirrored itself in a thousand conflicts – necessity versus freedom, matter versus spirit, sensuality versus asceticism, reason versus instinct, the real in contrast with the ideal – local engagements in a seemingly universal campaign. Strung in this field of force were Augustine and Albertus, Bacon and Milton, Darwin and Freud. These pairs of great men are mentioned not as antitheses but as illustrative examples. All the outstanding thinkers of Europe have been torn between the two poles, and sometimes famous men have incarnated the one and the other in head-on collision – as in the case of Huxley and Wilberforce. The crowning symbol of this divided mind was the Holy Roman Empire itself, with the Pope and the Emperor as the dual but inwardly irreconcilable apex, two persons on one throne, failing, alas, on earth to attain the perfect union of the three persons in heaven. Many a time have I stood with Chinese friends in our Western cathedrals – at Augsburg or Korčula, Chartres or Lincoln, delighting, like Henry Adams, to explain to them how the essential duality of the European soul found expression in the visible sharing of earthly power between lords spiritual and lords temporal. It is true, of course, that most of the theologians upheld an ultimate primacy of the Church, but century after century the King's lawyers stubbornly contested it.

Nothing of this kind existed in Chinese culture, for the emperor on earth was both priest and king. The Son of Heaven represented

[1] In *The Next Development in Man* (London, 1944), especially pp. 59, 61, 85, etc.

below the Pole Star in the heavens above, around which every star revolved. A famous passage in *Julius Caesar* describes this state of things:

> But I am constant as the northern star,
> Of whose true-fix'd and resting quality
> There is no fellow in the firmament.
> The skies are painted with un-number'd sparks,
> They are all fire and every one doth shine,
> But there's but one in all doth hold his place;
> So in the world—'tis furnish'd well with men . . .
> Yet in the number I do know but one
> That unassailable, holds on his rank,
> Unshaked of motion, and that I am he . . .

Such words could have been spoken by any Chinese emperor, the unitary head of church and state. It may, of course, be arguable that this 'schizophrenia' in Europe all through the centuries gave rise to a certain creative tension which was not present in Chinese society. It may well be that this perennial uneasiness was one of the great spiritual or intellectual factors which led to the rise of modern natural philosophy when the social situation became ripe for it; that remains to be investigated. What is sure, at any rate, is that Chinese culture attained sagely synthesis while adolescent Europe struggled on in the grip of ambivalence and contradiction.[1] Not until the time of Leibniz did the European spirit begin to be able to transcend the irreconcilable opposites of its youth – God and the

---

[1] What Alan Watts has written on this is deeply true – *The Way of Zen* (London, 1957), p. 175: 'Taoism, Confucianism and Zen Buddhism are expressions of a mentality which feels itself completely at home in this universe, and which sees man as an integral part of his environment. Human intelligence is not an imprisoned spirit from afar, but an aspect of the whole intricately balanced organism of the natural world, the principles of which were first explored in the *Book of Changes*. Heaven and earth are alike members of this organism, and Nature as much our father as our mother since the Tao by which it works is originally manifested in the Yang and the Yin – the male and female, positive and negative principles which in dynamic balance maintain the order of the world. The insight which lies at the root of the Far Eastern cultures is that opposites are relational, and so fundamentally harmonious. Conflict is always comparatively superficial, for there can be no ultimate conflict when the pairs of objects are mutually interdependent. Thus our stark divisions of spirit and nature, subject and object, good and evil artist, and medium, are quite foreign to these cultures'.

angels versus atoms and the void – creation against evolution – cassock and alb at odds with the divine nudity of Aphrodite. This argument does not imply that there were no basic psychological conflicts in Chinese civilization, for some of these are doubtless implicit in the human condition itself; but rather that conflicts within Western man were unduly heightened and intensified by a fundamentally unreconciled dualism, an unsolved contradiction, lying at the root of European culture itself. This is why it has so much yet to learn from China – and from India.

In any case, it is easy to see that the profound unitariness of Chinese culture not only favoured the acceptance of dialectical materialism as its own *philosophia perennis* in fully developed form, but was also very congruent with the conception of a one-party state. Traditional China had never been anything else. Though Taoists occasionally found their way to power, the real ruler through the ages was, as it were, the Confucian Party. This point is extremely important as it mirrors on the sociological side this philosophical, unitary, organic naturalism.

Moreover, Chinese intellectuals were all the more ready to accept dialectical materialism for it was something which in a way they themselves had generated. If one seeks for the origins of dialectical materialism in the West, one can get back to Hegel easily enough, but beyond Hegel there is only Leibniz and when one gets that far, it is not obvious where the further sources were. Of course, you can bring Plotinus into it (much to his surprise), but his philosophy, if organic, was hardly materialist, so it is well worth knowing that Leibniz himself was extremely interested in China. He wrote at least one book on that culture, the *Novissima Sinica*. He edited the Jesuit reports from China and was in extremely close touch with Jesuits living there, such as Joachim Bouvet; they supplied him with the Neo-Confucian commentaries on the classics as well as the classics themselves. Leibniz himself fortunately annotated copies of a number of books relating to Chinese thought, especially by dissentient Jesuits who did not agree with the usual Jesuit view about China, and from these notes we can see that if his own philosophical system was not primarily derived from Neo-Confucian organicism, he found in it much precious support and confirmation.[1]

THE ABSENCE OF METAPHYSICAL IDEALISM AND THEOLOGY

There is an obverse, of course, to all this and that is the absence of certain trends in China. Most conspicuous by its absence was any strong tradition of metaphysical idealism. Nothing in China corresponds to Berkeley and Bradley and nothing really corresponds to Plato, for it is only a *jeu d'esprit*, I think, to call Chuang Chou the Plato of China. In his literary manifestation this may pass, but the metaphysical ideas are just not there. I shed no tears about that because I am not a metaphysical idealist. It is true that from the end of the Sung onwards there was a wing of the Neo-Confucians which showed a strong tendency to metaphysical idealism, culminating in Wang Yang-Ming and the philosophers of the Ming period,[2] but even there it was, on the whole, I think, more mystical than metaphysical, since in general Chinese culture did not have that Greek inheritance of formal logic which led to metaphysical propositions in the strict sense.

Here again the Buddhist thinkers must not be forgotten, for many of their schools worked out extreme idealistic positions,[3] but whatever they did affected the general trend of Chinese thought, I submit, remarkably little. Buddhism in China was always really heterodox, powerful imperial support in certain dynasties notwithstanding, and all its conceptions – the total vanity of the world, the imperfectibility of human society, the salvation of the self by worship and almsgiving, the superiority of the monastic life of moderated asceticism – were decisively rejected by the *literati*. For them the world was not an illusion, good government and a society of justice and righteousness were

[1] *SCC*, Vol. 2, pp. 497ff., 500ff.

[2] Cf. F. G. Henke, *The Philosophy of Wang Yang-Ming* (Chicago, 1916), and, more recently, Fêng Yu-Lan, *A History of Chinese Philosophy*, translated by D. Bodde, Vol. 2 (Princeton, 1953), pp. 572ff.

[3] Cf. Fêng Yu-Lan, *loc. cit.*, Vol. 2, pp. 237ff., 293ff., 360ff.

feasible, the family with its moderated relations between the sexes was the right and natural way of living, and salvation could look after itself. By the same token there never appeared in China a powerful theological philosophy. The conception of the Creator-God was absent. I once had occasion to go into this in great detail because I was anxious to plumb to the bottom the absence of the conception of Laws of Nature in Chinese thought, and in the end I satisfied myself that it never spontaneously appeared.[1] Marcel Granet had indeed been right when he spoke about the Chinese conception of the universe as an order which positively excludes the notion of law. Leibniz's idea of a pre-established harmony was one of the most Chinese formulations which ever found itself incorporated in the procession of European philosophical thought.

NO PERSECUTION FOR OPINION'S SAKE

But if 'Laws of Nature' did not arise indigenously in the Chinese mind, perhaps some other consequences of the absence of a 'jealous' unitary personal God were highly advantageous. Take the question of persecution for opinion's sake. Let any unbiased enquirer look for himself and report if he can find in Chinese history anything corresponding to the Holy Inquisition. There were, no doubt, political censorships, such as the alarm and uneasiness at the Manchu Court, for instance, about writers who might be secretly supporting the Ming and working for a Ming restoration. In the eighteenth century A.D., as Goodrich has shown,[2]

[1] SCC, Vol. 2, pp. 518ff.; also, in preliminary form, 'Natural Law in China and Europe', Journal of the History of Ideas, **12**, 3 and 194 (1951); and abridged, 'Human Law and the Laws of Nature in China and the West' (Hobhouse Memorial Lecture, London, 1951). Interesting discussions continue still, however. Cf. D. Bodde in Harvard Journal of Asiatic Studies, **20**, 709 (1957).

[2] L. C. Goodrich, The Literary Inquisition of Chhien-Lung (Baltimore, 1935). The political battles between powerful eunuchs and Confucian reformers could be extremely fierce, as may be seen, for instance, by reading C. O. Hucker's study of the Tung-Lin movement of the late Ming in J. K. Fairbank, ed., Chinese Thought and Institutions (Chicago, 1957), p. 132. Moreover, intellectual originality could be dangerous in the more conventional periods, as may be seen by the sad case of a scholar named Li Chih (A.D. 1527-1602) who was driven to suicide in prison for a Confucian-Buddhist syncretism which a thousand years earlier would have

there was a good deal of draconic investigation of books involving some shocking and unhappy individual cases. But of persecution for theological opinion as we know it in Europe, with the whole background of Crusades against Muslims, Jews, and Albigensians, the Inquisition, and the manifold cruelties perpetrated by both sides 'for the good of their souls' in the wars of the Reformation and the Counter-Reformation, one simply cannot find any comparisons in China at all. I am not saying that the Buddhists were not interfered with from time to time. They were persecuted to the extent that thousands of monks and nuns were obliged to return to civilian life and even to marry. They were also injured by the enforced nationalization of some of the enormous Buddhist images, the bronze of which was melted down and made into coins. But the only religious persons ever burnt alive in China were some of the Buddhist monks of their own free will, for at times it was believed that suicide was the quickest and most efficacious way to attain Nirvana. The *literati* abhorred it.

Another phenomenon in European history for which it is difficult to find any counterpart in China, however one gropes amidst the superstitions which flourished in medieval times there as well as in other cultures, is the witchcraft mania.[1] For more than two centuries from the fifteenth to the eighteenth century A.D. Europe suffered a reign of terror in which unnumbered thousands of persons, notably but by no means exclusively old women, were burnt at the stake or tortured or killed in many other ways after condemnation as witches and sorcerers. This may have been just another aspect of the principle of religious persecution, but it had numerous features which have invited the attention of modern psycho-pathologists, and it

been in the height of fashion. On him one may read O. Franke in *Abhandlungen d. preuss. Akad. Wiss.* (Phil.-Hist. Kl.), 1938, No. 10. He was an enlightened freethinker, advocating many things which contemporary China unquestioningly accepts, such as the equality of the sexes and the free choice of partners in marriage, and has honour as a martyr of humanism. But such a case was exceptional.

[1] The best paper known to me on this subject is that of E. T. Withington, 'Dr. John Weyer and the Witch Mania', in C. Singer, ed., *Studies in the History and Method of Science* (Oxford, 1917; reprinted, London, 1955).

constitutes yet another cultural element which Western civilization face to face with modern Asia has some difficulty in explaining
away. It seems to have been a disease associated with the great
upheavals of the Renaissance, the Reformation, and the rise of
capitalism, for the earlier Middle Ages had been almost as free from
it as the nineteenth century. By contrast, the advantage of having
an entire magistracy vowed by long training to a humane
scepticism in matters of religion and magic will here be very
apparent. Precious philosophically the alogical and irrational
element at the heart of Christianity may have been, but it bore
inescapably the compensating curse that belief could take the place
of reason even on the judge's bench. Moreover, the popularity of
literary genres, which is not without relation to their social
environment, may show us something. Just as people today
delight in detective stories because they live in highly policed and
secure societies, tales of ghosts and 'occult' phenomena were very
popular in medieval China – precisely because few of the scholars
believed in them.

Indeed, the idea of religious persecution as understood by both
Catholics and Protestants in the West is, I think, truly absent from
Chinese history.[1] If it had been present, there could never have
been that extraordinary syncretism when in certain periods some

---

[1] This was really demonstrated in a classical work by J. J. M. de Groot, 'Sec-
tarianism and Religious Persecution in China', *Verhdl. d. Koninklijke Akad. Wet.
Amsterdam (Afd. Letterk.)* N. R. 4 (1903), Nos. 1 and 2 (continuous pagination),
though his own bias was in the opposite direction. The conception of heresy
(*yin ssu, hsieh shuo*) was not indeed totally absent from Chinese thinking, but it
was inextricably bound up with the fear of political subversion and popular
revolt against the ruling bureaucratic-feudal State. Thus the laws against sects
were really directed against secret societies, and a 'heretic' who abjured Confucianism or developed some aberrant form of Taoism or Buddhism was
indistinguishable from a rebel. Abundance of instances show that this 'alarm and
despondency' of the officials was perfectly justified; the burden of proof lay on
the sect to show that it was non-political. Yet in many ages there could be glad
acceptance of foreign religions and some were acclimatized successfully for
centuries – Zoroastrianism, Nestorian Christianity, Manichaeism, Islam, and
Israel, apart from the outstanding example of Buddhism itself. To sum up the
matter, the point at issue tended always to be political rather than philosophical,
and the *odium theologicum* of the West was by that token absent.

scholars went out of their way to dress up in Buddhist robes and a Confucian hat with a Taoist staff, and maintain that the *San Chiao*, the three religions, the three doctrines, were essentially parts of one and the same truth. Few in the West today are prepared to do that kind of thing even with the next chapel down the road.

Here again we come to a very important outcome at the present time, namely the emphasis on persuasion. In the last ten years in China, I do not know how many man-hours or man/woman-hours or years have been spent attending meetings. The extent to which the Chinese have gone in for meetings has probably never been surpassed in the history of the world since the Early Church. I think it has been done because of this deeply-rooted feeling that you cannot make people really enthusiastic about anything against their will. In fact, so far as I can see, life in the Soviet Union never embodied the profusion of rectification meetings common to every social unit in China; in every laboratory, in every railway junction, in every workshop, these group meetings have been going on. What I have heard from a number of Western friends who have participated in these meetings leaves no doubt that the result has been much greater co-operation and much greater mutual understanding than is probably ever achieved in the working-together groups of our own society.[1]

DECEMBER 25TH OR JULY 14TH?

Four times in history China was offered the possibility of adopting organized Christianity: once in the eighth century A.D., when the Syrian Nestorians came; once in the thirteenth century A.D., when there was a Franciscan Archbishop of Cambaluc; once again in the seventeenth century A.D., in the brilliant age of the Jesuit Mission; and lastly in the nineteenth century A.D., when the Thai-Phing rebels drew part of their inspiration from a form of

[1] Anyone who would like to go further into this might read what W. J. H. Sprott, Professor of Psychology at Nottingham, has written in his book *Human Groups* (London, 1958). He spent considerable time in China a few years ago, studying this from the aspect of group therapy.

Protestantism. But it always failed, and the fact must be faced by Westerners that the Christian religion in its organized forms has been decisively rejected by Chinese culture. As Antonio Banfi has put it,[1] this necessarily followed from the highly organic structure of Chinese humanistic morality, which could not but view with distaste a religion placing so tragic an accent upon transcendence, and therefore inevitably so dogmatic and ecclesiastical. What the Jesuits offered of modern science was enthusiastically received, and though for them the scientific contacts were only a means to an end, they succeeded fully in acclimatizing Galileo and Harvey while utterly failing in their principal aim, the transplantation of Augustine and Aquinas. The Chinese, with their usual acumen, saw through the Jesuit pretensions completely and realized that the modern science of the Renaissance was not something essentially Western, but something essentially new.[2] They also realized that it had nothing intrinsically to do with Christianity.[3] The religion and theology of Europe could not be regarded as 'superior' doctrines; they had developed, no doubt, in the same civilization as modern science, but this was a relation of accidental historical contiguity and not one of necessary cause and effect. Moreover, as time went on, the behaviour of the Western powers, with all its elements of imperialistic bullying and racial pride, made the preaching of missionaries seem more and more systematically hypocritical. The last straw in this process has been added in our own time by the self-caricature of its *mores* and modes of

---

[1] *Comprendre*, **19**, 21 (1958).

[2] This point is elaborated in detail in SCC, Vol. 3, pp. 448ff. See also J. Needham, *Chinese Astronomy and the Jesuit Mission; an Encounter of Cultures* (London, 1958).

[3] The implicit logic of the Jesuit approach was that modern science was better than medieval science, and that only Christendom could have produced it; the Chinese should therefore become part of Christendom. The *non sequitur* was that a unique historical circumstance (the rise of modern science in a civilization with a particular religion) cannot prove a necessary concomitance. Religion was not the only factor in which Europe differed from Asia. In the actual historical and ideological genesis of science and modern science, Israel and Christianity, and for that matter Hellenism, too, were no doubt very much concerned, but historical genesis is not the same thing as intrinsic inseparability. Once the historical process had come about, other world-views could be just as compatible with science as Christianity ever was, if not more so, as in the case of Taoism.

life which the West has offered to Asia, that mixture of sex and sadism characteristic of its cheap films and books.

Such was the negative effect of Europe on China. But if the West could not make clear and sincere the message of December 25th, that of July 14th was a very different matter. Christianity has been well called 'the grandmother of Bolshevism', but that ancestry had been part of a particular historical process, and philosophically other grandparents or 'foster-grandparents', for example, Confucianism or Taoism, could qualify in other parts of the world. The revolutionary socialism of the great European bourgeois revolutions, from the Levellers at Burford Bridge to the Sans-Culottes storming the Bastille, went over into Chinese culture without the slightest obstacle because it had to do more clearly with the fundamental needs of men incarnate in their material being. This was the great positive effect. On such common ground China and all Asia could accept European influence unhesitatingly, for Europe, too, was giving something up – its own heritage of medieval feudal and capitalist oppression, as well as the beliefs connected therewith.[1] Besides, in the course of time, a more enlightened West would be ready to accept Chinese influence once again, as it had done with such effect in the eighteenth century.[2]

All the pioneers of modern China were marching in this demonstration. One of the greatest of Sir Thomas More's successors was Khang Yu-Wei, who in his *Ta Thung Shu* (Book

[1] This has been seen by J. R. Levenson in a brief but most acute paper, 'Western Religion and the Decay of Traditional China; the Intrusion of History on Judgments of Value', *Sinologica*, 4, 14 (1954). He reprinted it in his book, *Confucian China and its Modern Fate; the Problem of Intellectual Continuity* (London, 1958), pp. 117 ff. This work is full of ingenious studies and valuable insights, yet it fails altogether in its main objective, namely, to show that contemporary China has lost its roots in the past. Indeed, in its anxiety to magnify Western influence on Chinese thinking at all costs, Levenson's work runs grave risk of being described as the last refuge of the doctrine of Western intellectual superiority.

[2] Europe's discovery of a morality without supernaturalism, a chronology without a flood, and a cosmology without any crystalline spheres is an oft-told story which need not be repeated here. But I shall never forget the impassioned telling of it long ago at a lecture in Cambridge, to which Dr E. R. Hughes came armed with the heavy artillery of *Confucius Sinarum Philosophus* in folio.

of the Great Togetherness) sketched a 'utopia' extraordinarily far-seeing in its structure and imbued with many traits characteristic of the Chinese tradition as well as of the modern scientific world-view.[1] The greater Sun Yat-Sen, that improbable medical revolutionary to whom I have already referred, did his best in his Three Principles to put socialism into Chinese terms.[2] It is surely needless to recall that at that time the influence of the Russian Revolution on Chinese thinking was extremely powerful. And, indeed, until 1927 the Kuomintang was a real positive force, even if only semi-conscious; it did a great deal to modernize the country, to stamp out abuses, and to continue the tradition of public works and public ownership of industrial enterprises. Only after the crisis of that year was it fully captured by the landowner-banker-comprador group, who found it much more profitable to engage in financial speculation abroad than to develop their own country. But this only postponed the inevitable conclusion, for what the Chinese people fundamentally appreciated of Europe was the ideal of liberty, equality, and fraternity, not the theology of a Church too often, alas, subservient to the powers that be.[3] Moreover, the merit of Marxism (or, as it was called by its founding fathers, 'scientific socialism') was, in Chinese eyes, that although it had originated in a particular historical situation in

[1] This work was conceived and first drafted in 1884 and 1885, first printed (in part) in 1913, and first completely published in 1935 (reprinted in Peking in 1956). An excellent but abridged translation by L. G. Thompson, *The One-World Philosophy of Khang Yu-Wei* (London, 1958), is now available.

[2] Besides the paper by Scalapino & Schiffrin mentioned already on p. 37 above, see H. Schiffrin on Sun Yat-Sen's land policy in *Journal of Asian Studies*, **16** 549, (1957). On that great man there are many books, but reference to L. Sharman, *Sun Yat-Sen, his Life and its Meaning; a Critical Biography* (New York, 1934), will have to be enough here. A *Source-Book of Sun Yat-Sen's Political and Social Ideals* was collected and translated by Hsü Shih-Lien (Los Angeles, 1933).

[3] One might find parallels within the European orbit itself. In his recent book, *The Greek East and the Latin West; a Study in the Christian Tradition* (Oxford, 1959), Philip Sherrard, writing of the time of Korais in the early nineteenth century, says: 'Thus the union with Western Europe which the Greek East had so energetically rejected at the close of the Byzantine period was at last to be accomplished, not any longer in Christian terms, but in those of the secular and temporal ideals of the modern West.'

Western Europe, its doctrine, like that of physical science itself, was intrinsically universal, not tied to any particular civilization, and capable of illuminating and analyzing the social history of the Chinese themselves. And so both Chinese and Westerners could go forward on an equal and mutually appreciative basis, both working to end the oppression of the past in all its forms, 'neither afore nor after other', 'without any difference or inequality'.[1]

CHINA AND THE HISTORY OF LAW

All this was bound to have a great effect on the Chinese conceptions of law. One can well understand why there was no feeling of outrage when the previous Kuomintang code, after all a very artificial importation from the West, was swept away and replaced by more popular laws. In fact, throughout Chinese history there was a great dislike of codification and a strong aversion to legal principle.[2] The devotion of Roman law, for

[1] On the vitally important mental attitudes here involved, the controversy between Umberto Campagnolo and Alioune Diop which has recently been going on in *Comprendre*, **19**, 7ff., 9ff., 157ff. (1958), is well worth reading. Campagnolo voices a widely held view when he states as a dilemma that either the great historical civilizations are immiscible and irreducible individuals, in which case they can never meet, or they are destined to transcend themselves in a world culture, in which case no one can know what this will be. Campagnolo escapes from this by maintaining that one of the great civilizations possesses in its original intuition and principles the means which permit it to understand and to estimate the others, and to lead them to estimate themselves according to its own scale of values. This is the 'civilization of the universal' which has developed only in Europe (and by extension, in America) and upon which devolves the historic mission of accomplishing the ethnic unification of the world. To this Diop replies that such a doctrine is nothing but racialism in its most rarefied, insidious, and Sunday-go-to-meeting form. The civilization of the universal cannot for a moment, he says, be confused with the civilization of the West, but must necessarily arise from the contributions of all peoples; and the fact that we cannot yet know its features is not an argument for denying that it will come. Needless to say, I am fully in sympathy with Diop. The conception of the 'chosen people', God's elect, which Europeans and Americans have transferred to themselves from ancient Israel by way of the link between puritanism and capitalism in the early phases of Western technological development, is still working great evil in the world.

[2] This is explained more fully in *SCC*, Vol. 2, pp. 521ff.

instance, to highly abstract formulations cannot be paralleled at any time in China. There was a profound belief that every case ought to be judged in the light of the concrete circumstances, i.e., on its own merits. I am not, of course, saying that there was never any codification of law. On the contrary, there were jurists in every century from the Han onwards and many of them compiled great collections of law cases; moreover, there were official codes, of course, in each dynasty. Yet on the whole they never played anything like the part (many people would say the 'sublime part') of the Justinian code and the other great legal institutions of Europe. Furthermore, the idea of equity, if that is the right way to phrase it, was much more important in China than the idea of positive law. Expressions like *summa lex, summa injuria*, would have been inconceivable in traditional Chinese society. Arthur Waley once excellently remarked that in China in the Middle Ages no magistrate, having made what he knew to be an unjust judgment, would have descended from his bench congratulating himself on having faithfully applied the law of the land.[1] This was not a characteristic of Chinese jurisprudence, nor was there any delight in legal fictions. Similarly, Chinese medieval society was not characterized by great addiction to litigation. People chiefly kept out of the way of the nosphomeric civil magistrate as much as they could, and did not enjoy taking cases to be judged in civil actions such as the West delighted in. Advocates and pleaders were therefore scarce, and the magistrates' consciences were counsel for the defence. Such differences in the conception of law in China and the West do seem to help in explaining the changes of the present day.

CHINA AND THE HISTORY OF SCIENCE

Finally we come to the last question which I wish to raise, namely, the position of Chinese culture in the history of science and technology. Only the study of the social, intellectual and economic system will explain the remarkable development of science, pure

[1] A. Waley, *The Life and Times of Pai Chü-I* (London, 1949), p. 141.

and applied, in China in ancient and medieval times; and the failure, or, if you like, the absence, of the development of *modern* science there since the time of Galileo at the beginning of the seventeenth century A.D. One may say, broadly speaking, that Chinese science and technology were very much more advanced than those of Europe (apart from the Hellenistic wave of brilliant theoretical formulation) between the third century B.C. and the fifteenth century A.D., but after that Renaissance Europe began to take the lead. Indeed, in Galileo's time the technique of scientific discovery may be said to have been itself discovered, with the result that the unified world of modern science came into being, common to all men and liberated from the ethnic stamp which had qualified all forms of medieval science and technology. As I have said elsewhere[1] one must understand clearly that Renaissance Europe did not give rise to 'European science', but to universally valid *modern* science, in which men and women of all cultures can freely participate. The fact that this break-through took place in Europe and in Europe only is not proof of any specially privileged quality of the 'Faustian soul', as the Germanic mystagogues used to maintain, nor is it an argument for conferring upon European civilization a superior rank as the 'culture of the universal' as certain writers today still like to maintain. For until it has been demonstrated that the concrete historical development of Europe, the form of its feudalism, the needs of its growing mercantilism and industrialization, the prior impulsions and facilitations of its intellectual history from the pre-Socratic Greeks onwards, and other similar factors, will not explain in an adequate manner the 'miracle of Galileo', we have no right to appeal to mysterious predestinations or gifts of the European spirit as the explanation of the origin and growth of modern science. And in view of the great achievements of non-European peoples on which this modern science was built, we have every reason for not doing this. As for China, the problem remains: why did the Chinese society

[1] *Comprendre*, **12**, 132 (1954); cf. *SCC*, Vol. 3, pp. 448ff. For a well-stated Chinese view of this see Wu Shao-Fêng, 'L'Europe Créatrice', *Comprendre*, **19**, 213 (1958).

of the eighth century A.D. favour science as compared with Western society, and that of the eighteenth century A.D. inhibit it?

What happened at the Renaissance in Europe, the immense rise of modern science after the time of Galileo and the perfection of the method of the mathematization of hypotheses, had profound effects upon the relations of the peoples of East and West. We know only too well the results of it. We know how the Western standard of life was powerfully raised by modern technology, and also how bad it was for Westerners to be granted those two or three hundred years of military dominance in which they could so easily overawe all other cultures.[1] But if the world can avoid self-destruction by the unimaginable powers which modern physics has unleashed, it can benefit almost unimaginably by them. Behind this question of why the rise of *modern* science took place only in Europe, and did not occur in East Asian civilization in spite of so many great Chinese achievements in the past in the scientific, mathematical, and technological fields, lie all the problems of the nature and development of Chinese society.

We have already had occasion to make certain suggestions as to why nothing corresponding to the Renaissance took place there. The whole city-state motif was absent in China from the start. The merchant interest, of such cardinal importance for the rise of modern science in the West, was systematically suppressed in China. Then there were the ideological factors, on the one hand the assembly of deified ancestors, and on the other hand the personal creator-god, whose rational decrees men thought they could spell out haltingly in their own mathematical language;[2] or again on the one hand the indwelling Tao of things which made them spontaneously co-operate, on the other the assumption of atomistic impacts and mechanical

[1] Moreover, as J. Romein has well said in *Comprendre*, **19,** 91 (1958): 'from their temporary technical superiority Westerners wrongly inferred a perennial Chinese technical inferiority'.

[2] See the references given in note 1 on p. 73.

propulsions.[1] Natural science in its modern form seems to have needed a certain heuristic naïveté which Chinese natural wisdom lacked.

Such was the first question which prompted me to devote the rest of my life to preparing a comprehensive treatise on the history of science, scientific thought, and technology in China. Afterwards I came to realize that behind this there was another question at least equally important: why, before the Renaissance, in the period from about 200 B.C. down to about A.D. 1400 or A.D. 1450, was China often so far ahead of Europe? This also has to be answered: why was bureaucratic feudalism so much more efficient than Hellenistic imperialism or medieval Western feudalism in applying science to human affairs – very often, in a way, applying a theoretical science that did not exist? This paradox is rather nice, but one can give many examples to illustrate it, not all by any means in the technological field. Let us leave on one side the famous inventions of printing, gunpowder, and the magnetic compass, so justly celebrated by Francis Bacon. I have already referred to the mastery of the technique of cast iron, the obtaining and handling of iron in the fused state. In Europe no one knew any cast iron until about A.D. 1380. In China, however, they had been habitually making agricultural tools of it as far back as the second century B.C. I cannot, of course, stop here to explain how it was done. I think we know.[2] It is only one outstanding example of how far China was ahead of the West technically in those early centuries. Equally striking is the fact that in the absence of deductive geometry as developed by Euclid and Apollonius in the West, it was in China and not in Europe that long before the Renaissance the inventions of the equatorial

[1] *SCC*, Vol. 2, pp. 279ff. It is highly significant that while theories of atomism never 'caught on' in China, though continually introduced in association with Indian Buddhist thought, the Chinese developed primitive but quite clear forms of wave-theory, especially in relation to the influence of Yang and Yin forces. This is discussed in detail in *SCC*, Vol. 4, Pt. I, but reference may also be made to J. Needham & K. Robinson, 'Les Ondes et les Particules dans la Pensée Scientifique Chinoise', *Sciences* (Paris, 1960). Similarly, the idea of 'action at a distance' aroused no difficulties in Chinese scientific thinking and was accepted by everyone.

[2] See the references given in note I on p. 44.

mounting for the telescope[1] and of the mechanical clock[2] were made. This latter is particularly extraordinary, since China has so often been pictured as a 'timeless' agrarian civilization.

One point which may be very significant is that some of these medieval inventions were closely connected with the bureaucratic character of the culture. As instances one might mention the seismograph[3] and the rain-gauges and snow-gauges.[4] In a closely knit bureaucratic structure, an élite society where there was a high degree of organization and foresight, even though feudal, it was desirable indeed to be able to know if and where an earthquake had occurred, in order to be sure to send relief and also perhaps troops to the area which had been severely affected. This was clearly the case in the second century A.D. when the ancestor of all seismographs was put into operation by Chang Hêng. Equally, the rain-gauges and the snow-gauges are interesting from this point of view because it was necessary to be forewarned if there were going to be serious floods, and we know from eleventh- and twelfth-century mathematical books, which give problems about the shape of rain-gauges, that they were quite widely used, probably established among the western foothills bordering on the Tibetan plateau, to tell how the rainfall and the snowfall were shaping. Another example about which my collaborators and I have recently written at length[5] concerns a very remarkable geodetic survey, the meridian arc established by Chinese expedi-

[1] *SCC*, Vol. 3, pp. 367ff., and J. Needham, 'The Peking Observatory in A.D. 1280 and the Development of the Equatorial Mounting', in A. Beer, ed., *Vistas in Astronomy* (Stratton Presentation Volume), **1**, 67 (1955).

[2] *SCC*, Vol. 4 Pt. 2, pp. 435 ff., also J. Needham, L. Wang, & D. J. de S. Price in *Nature*, **177**, 600 (1956); and *Heavenly Clockwork; the Great Astronomical Clocks of Mediaeval China* (Cambridge, 1960). See also my 'The Missing Link in Horological History; a Chinese Contribution', *Proc. Roy. Soc. A.*, **250**, 147 (1959), (Wilkins Lecture at the Royal Society).

[3] *SCC*, Vol. 3, pp. 626ff.

[4] *SCC*, Vol. 3, pp. 471ff.

[5] *SCC*, Vol. 3, p. 292ff., but much more fully in the paper by A. Beer, Ho Ping-Yü, Lu Gwei-Djen, J. Needham, E. G. Pulleyblank, & G. I. Thompson, 'An eighth-century Meridian Line; I-Hsing's Chain of Gnomons and the Pre-History of the Metric System', *Vistas in Astronomy*, **4**, 3 (1961).

tions sent forth in the year A.D. 723, which made measurements for two or three years and then combined the results. This was under the supervision of the Astronomer-Royal, Nankung Yüeh, and an outstanding Buddhist monk and mathematician, I-Hsing. This arc was undoubtedly the most remarkable piece of organized field work in the whole of the Middle Ages, for it ran from the borders of Mongolia right down to Indo-China, a distance of some 2,500 kilometres, with about nine stations along it at which systematic observations were made of the summer and winter solstice shadows and polar altitudes. I doubt whether in any other medieval culture it would have been possible to imagine or to carry out such a highly organized scientific survey. It therefore clearly deserves remembrance, and it was certainly associated with the bureaucratic character of that feudal society.

China today is recovering these past achievements and much work on the history of science is going on. There is a great enthusiasm there for science as the indispensable means of raising the Asian standard of life to equality with the rest of the world. But Chinese people are also beginning to be very conscious of the great discoveries, observations, and inventions made by their ancestors. They are getting to know about facts which the dust-storms of history have hidden for centuries, and which historians of the modern West have not always been happy to uncover.[1] Is it not important for the disinherited thinkers and technicians of Asia to realize that though the first complete Western descriptions of parhelic phenomena (mock suns, haloes, and arcs, caused by ice crystals in the upper atmosphere) were given in the seventeenth

---

[1] Thus the Jesuits knew about the sand-driven wheel-clocks used in the Ming but said remarkably little about them in their despatches home, and that not very complimentary; see *Heavenly Clockwork*, pp. 155ff. I well remember that when an exhibition of the history of printing in England to celebrate a Gutenberg centenary was being prepared, a suggestion that some specimens of earlier Chinese movable-type printing might be included met with a somewhat chilly reception. And typical of the approach of some Western scholars was the remark of an eminent historian of magnetism concerning the eleventh-century description of the needle-compass by Shen Kua: 'there is no immediately apparent ground on which this can be discredited'. The reference will be found in *SCC*, Vol. 4, Pt. 1, p. 250.

century A.D., every single component of the complex displays had been observed and named by Chinese astronomers a full thousand years before? [1] Should they not take legitimate pride in the fact that the combination of eccentric, connecting-rod, and piston-rod, used in every steam engine since Watt and in every internal combustion engine, first occurs not in the designs of the engineers of the Italian Renaissance, nor in Leonardo, nor in the Germans or Bohemians who preceded him, certainly not in the Alexandrians, but in the metallurgical water-powered blowing engines described by Wang Chên about A.D. 1300? [2] You may now even find little books of pictures for school children explaining to them about Chang Hêng and his seismograph, or about Tshai Lun's first-century A.D. invention of paper, or Pi Shêng's eleventh-century creation of movable type; how the 'Cardan' suspension goes back to Ting Huan about A.D. 180,[3] and the 'Pascal' triangle to Chu Shih-Chieh in A.D. 1303.[4] All these achievements are well established by sinological research. Thus Westerners should realize that science is not regarded in China as something for which the Chinese should feel themselves beholden to the generosity and kindness of Christian missionaries, something with no roots in their own culture. On the contrary, it has very great and illustrious roots, and the Chinese are becoming more and more conscious of them. If the society of the Chinese Middle Ages had been so lacking in freedom, so despotic, as some would have us believe, the innumerable inventions and discoveries of those ages would be perfectly inexplicable; nor could one see how the lead over Europe could have been maintained for so long. Stability perhaps, but where was the 'societal stagnation' which some of our pundits find exemplified in medieval Chinese culture?

[1] *SCC*, Vol. 3, pp. 474ff., and with much more detail in Ho Ping-Yü & J. Needham, 'Ancient Chinese Observations of Solar Haloes and Parhelia', *Weather*, **14**, 124 (1959).
[2] The evidence is assembled in *SCC*, Vol. 4, Pt. 2, pp. 369ff.
[3] See *SCC*, Vol. 4, Pt. 2, pp. 228ff.
[4] See *SCC*, Vol. 3, pp. 133ff.

EPILOGUE

It has been my aim in the foregoing pages to provide a background for thought on contemporary China, seen through the eyes of one student of the history and culture of that great civilization. I have no wish to minimize in any way the extraordinary improvements in the lot of the 'old hundred names' which have been effected by the present Chinese government and under the leadership of the Communist Party. At the same time, its work can hardly be understood by Westerners unless they bear in mind certain age-old features of Chinese culture of which too often they are lamentably ignorant. Indeed, contemporary Chinese writers themselves, with the laudable aim of demonstrating the profound renewal and rebirth of their country, sometimes tend to denigrate their own past, whether by emphasizing dark aspects such as the subjection of women or the rapacity of landlords, or by under-valuing the philosophy or art of former ages. This is only to cut off the branch on which they are sitting. The fact is that the rest of the world needs to learn, with all humility, not only from contemporary China but from the China of all time, for in Chinese wisdom and experience there are medicines for many diseases of the spirit and indispensable elements of the future philosophy of humanity.

3

THE CHINESE CONTRIBUTION
TO SCIENTIFIC HUMANISM

First published in *Free World*, 1942

Probably most Westerners hardly realize the extent to which Chinese thought had advanced to the position of scientific humanism long before our own time, handicapped as it was by the complete failure of Chinese civilization to develop modern science unaided. Of medieval technology and medieval science there was plenty, and in ancient philosophy the Chinese stood side by side with the Greeks. Three or four hundred years ago the level of civilization and the standard of life in China probably surpassed that of Western Europe considerably; the rise of modern science and all that that implies has brought about the difference.

China has long had the *san chiao*, the three doctrines, side by side, but only one of them, Buddhism, was a true other-worldly religion. The other two, Confucianism and Taoism, were fundamentally philosophies. Confucianism degenerated into social conventionality, rising periodically to peaks of the numinous when governors or magistrates held sacrificial ceremonies in the sage's honour in the *wên miao* or Confucian temple which every city has; Taoism degenerated by alliance with ancient central Asiatic shamanism into fortune-telling and occultism, with a pantheon of gods artificially created to combat the Buddhists. But in their philosophical forms they are vital for the understanding of Chinese thought.

Confucianism, as appears from the classics, such as the *Conversations and Discourses* and the work of great Confucian scholars such as Mencius, is the most social-minded and humanistic doctrine that any part of the world has ever known. The Confucians were interested primarily in social justice (allowing, of course, for their markedly feudal background), in society and the relations between rulers and ruled, the state and the family, etc. 'If the state was as it should be,' said Kung Fu Tzu, 'I should not be always trying to change it.' Concerning celestial matters, the gods and spirits, he was very reluctant to speak. When specifically asked about them he replied: 'First learn to live at peace with your fellow men; then you may ask about the gods and spirits.' Of all the systems of the numinous which humanity has seen, Confucianism has the least possible admixture of the supernatural, which is why the *wên miao* has more charm than any other type of religious building in the world.

One of the profoundest effects of Confucianism was exerted ultimately on the West as well as on China. In the formative period of Confucian philosophy, about the fourth and third centuries B.C., there was much discussion about the fundamental nature of man's spirit. Some schools, such as that of the Legalists, said it was evil and could only be schooled by the draconic laws of a drastic prince. The Confucians, however, maintained it was basically good. Thus, since Confucianism won the day in China, the relations between Pelagius and Augustine were precisely reversed. Ultimately, the philosopher Hsün Tzu adopted the reasonable view that it was partly bad and partly good, or as we might say today, that it embodies both evolutionary regressive egoistic tendencies and evolutionarily progressive altruistic and co-operative tendencies. But from the heuristic point of view, Mencius and Pelagius are much better than Shang Yang and Augustine, since an optimistic belief about the possibilities of man lies at the base of all progressive social policies. Now few people in the West realize that the Confucian classics were translated into Latin by the Jesuits about A.D. 1680, came to the West, and were read with avidity by all the great forerunners of the French Revolution, by Voltaire, Rousseau, d'Alembert, Diderot, etc. From their comments, which we can read today, we know how stimulated they were.

In some ways, however, Confucianism was all too humanistic; though humanist, it was anti-scientific. It simply had no interest in the world outside human society. It discouraged such interest. Hence the great revolt of the Taoist philosophers, the shadowy Lao Tzu and the brilliant and lovable Chuang Tzu. The Taoists had a great deal in common with the Epicureans of middle Mediterranean antiquity; Lucretius spoke the same language as the Taoists. Wishing to attain perfect calm of mind and protection from all fear (like the ataraxy of the Epicureans) they withdrew from human society and meditated on mountain tops in order to reach some understanding of Nature. Wishing to achieve a material immortality, or at least an extreme prolongation of life, they undertook all kinds of curious regimens, and were willing to make experiments with diets and drugs – in this way alchemy, the parent of all modern chemistry, was born. Wishing an ultimate benefit to mankind, they took no interest in any immediate measures, for they felt in their bones that however much the busybody Confucians might run to and fro, human society would never come to much until human beings acquired some understanding of that vast environing world in which they were set.

For the Taoists the world was *tzu-jan*, that is, spontaneously originating. 'The way of animals depends upon man, the way of man depends on that of heaven, the way of heaven depends on the Tao, and the Tao came into being by itself.' Its spontaneity, its naturalness, not subject to any god or gods, resembles the Epicurean

> *quae bene cognita si teneas, natura videtur*
> *libera continuo dominis privata superbis*
> *ipsa sua per se sponte omnia dis agere expers.*

> Thus Nature loosed from every haughty lord
> And forthwith free, is seen to have done all things
> Herself and through herself of her own accord
> Rid of all gods.

Heuristically this assertion has always been one of the prerequisites of science. The Tao was the Way in which all Nature worked, not merely, as it was for the Confucians, the Way in which men ought to behave within human society. We see this, for instance, in Chuang Tzu's story of the butcher of Prince Hui, who could cut up a bullock with five strokes of his knife, and on being asked how he did it, replied that he had studied all his life the Tao of the joints and muscles. 'Confucius walks within human society,' said Chuang Tzu. 'I walk outside it.'

The Taoists inveighed in many a diatribe against 'knowledge', but they meant only the scholastic knowledge of the Confucians, 'making clever distinctions between princes and grooms'. Much of the passivity which they counselled was greatly misunderstood by subsequent generations. They praised what they called the 'valley spirit', the 'eternal feminine'; and in this passivity they were surely groping after something of that intellectual humility which the scientist must have in the face of nature. The Taoists urged that all preconceived ideas should be put aside, and that no natural phenomenon, however trivial or however disgusting, should be regarded as outside the range of the natural philosopher's vision. 'The sage,' says Kuan Tzu, 'is like Heaven, covering all things impartially, and again he is like Earth, impartially bearing up everything.' That the Taoists were ultimately looking for the means of controlling Nature also emerges from all their books – thus Kuan Tzu says: 'The sage follows after things, in order that he may control them.' If the Taoists often fell into magical ways of thought, supposing that they had found short cuts to the control of Nature, little else could have been expected in their age.

Indeed, apart from the empirical experiments of the alchemists, the Taoists never developed any valid method of investigating Nature. Hence the wearisome number-mysticism of a book such as the *Huai Nan Tzu*, everything running in set groups such as the four directions, the five grains, the six openings of the body, the nine tones, etc., with permutations and combinations in a great deal of fanciful arithmetic. Hence, much later on, the sarcasms of Wang Yang-Ming, who said he had derived no further insight into plants from the injunction to meditate in front of a bamboo for several days. Feeling no more enlightened than at the beginning, he betook himself to idealist metaphysics.

All in all, there are good grounds for saying that China is one of the original homes of scientific humanism. Anciently the humanism was supplied by the Confucians and the science by the Taoists.

But China's ancient philosophical schools are far from completing the story. There is hardly space in so short an article to mention the schools of Hui Tzu and the logicians whose relations with primitive science were very important, or the school of Mo Tzu who would have been entirely at home with those in our own time who emphasize the social duties and significance of science. Neither achieved any lasting success, but the Mohists combined the Confucian passion for social justice and order with the Taoist interest in Nature and human control over her.

It may be better to refer to aspects of much later Chinese thought. The commonly-accepted Western idea that Chinese civilization was stagnant for two thousand years evaporates as soon as one gets to know anything about Chinese history, though there is a sense in which the system of bureaucratic feudalism which developed in China brought about a cyclic series of dynastic successions. In the late Han Dynasty (about A.D. 100) China produced a scientific thinker of exceptional calibre, Wang Chhung. In his book, *The Balance* (for weighing contemporary opinions), he conducted a lonely but determined fight against the superstition of the age, such as the idea, contained in the unorthodox or Wei classics, that storms and catastrophes were visited upon mankind by Heaven as the result of some sin, or perhaps a failure of the Emperor to sit in a certain way, or to wear clothes of a certain colour at the appointed time in his minutely regulated life. Wang Chhung was, in fact, a great sceptic and a great crusader against magic.

Five centuries later, in the Thang Dynasty, China reached one of the greatest summits in the history of her arts and literature, but it was reserved for the following dynasty, the Sung (about the eleventh century A.D.), to produce a great school of natural philosophers. In the immortal book of Shen Kua, *Dream Pool* *Essays*, many natural phenomena are chronicled objectively for the first time, for example, the directive property and the declination of the magnet. At this time, too, gunpowder was widely used, before the appearance of Genghis Khan in the West.

But the philosophical interest centres round the school of Chu Hsi. The description of him as a kind of Chinese Herbert Spencer eight centuries before the Victorians is not entirely beside the mark. The Sung Confucians were stimulated largely, it seems, by the Buddhists, whose clear, though fantastic, world-scheme made Confucians very conscious of the absence of a world-scheme in their own philosophy. The key-word in Chu Hsi is *li* not *tao*; *li* today is often translated 'principle' but it originally meant the veinous pattern on a piece of jade. It has therefore the undertone of pattern, reminding us of the organismic patterns about which a Whitehead might speak. Chu Hsi, somewhat reminiscent of Aristotle, had a well worked-out cosmology, including processes such as centrifugal force, and he came near to an energy theory. The quality of his thought may be gauged by the fact that he gave the correct explanation of fossils, some 400 hundred years before Leonardo da Vinci did so in the West.

Nor does the process stop until modern times. When in the seventeenth century A.D. the Manchus conquered the Ming dynasty, among many officials who would not serve the new foreign government was one Wang Chhuan-Shan. He retired to the mountains and wrote many books. Modern scholars have discovered in his philosophy an approximation to, and premonitions of, dialectical materialism.

In general, then, we may say that Chinese scientific humanism, though all its achievements were made before there was any modern science in China at all, rested on two main bases. It never separated man from nature, and never thought of man apart from social man.

One especially outstanding instance of this is found in the concentration of the Taoists on change. Outdoing Heraclitus, they distinguished between *pien* and *hua*; 'The sage', they said, 'changes but is not transformed'. This rebellion against formal logic foreshadowed the revolt to which natural science was to be driven two thousand years later and its elaboration of a dialectical logic. In Chuang Tzu, indeed, we find a statement of a kind of biological evolution theory, while the Great Appendix of the *I Ching*, and the Book of Rites, have a full-fledged statement of social evolution.

The fundamental basis in modern science for scientific humanism is in fact the evolutionary view of the world. Though popularly associated largely with the biological sciences, it arises not only there but in all the inorganic sciences as well, since the earth went through a vast series of changes before any life appeared on it. There is a sense in which we may still employ the medieval fancy that man is a microcosm of the world. Our beings are themselves parts of social wholes, but beneath the bodily level they are composed of a hierarchy of levels, the organ in the body, the cell in the organ, the nucleus and other organelles in the cell, the colloidal micelle within these, and still farther down the organic molecules within these again, coming eventually to the constituent atoms and the physical particles, the protons, electrons, neutrons, positrons, etc., circling eternally in those minute but relatively vast solar systems which are the atoms of the chemical elements. This is one fundamental datum. The other is that we know how these levels form a succession in time. There were physical particles before there were chemical atoms, and of these there were small stable ones before there were large unstable ones. There were chemical atoms before there were molecules and many an age elapsed before atoms sufficiently complex to build living matter appeared. And then, when once that change had occurred, the stage was set for the vast evolutionary succession leading from the simplest bacteria and protozoa up to man.

Only one principle can be found running through this enormous scheme; we may call it a rise in the level of organization; a progressive appearance of ever more highly integrated wholes. Such a picture, corresponding on the philosophical side to the thought of many modern philosophers (such as Marx and Engels, Whitehead and Alexander and Smuts), leaves little room for supernaturalism in our estimate of man. Of the nature of the 'force' behind the process, of what happened when at the beginning 'energy of so many billion units was poured into space-time', of why the process should have started and whether or when it will stop, we can expect to know little or nothing. But the status of man in this philosophy, unlike what it was in the old-fashioned mechanical materialisms, is a high one. He is, indeed, the highest of creatures, not to be reduced to, or understood wholly in terms of, any of the lower levels; and in his societies he looks towards higher levels still, levels to which as yet he has not in fact attained.

We see now that with two concepts alone, those of energy (for matter-mass is now regarded as simply a special form of energy), and organization (*li* at various levels of its manifestation) our whole world can be built up. We are much less sure about what is going on in other parts of the universe. But it seems now as if the existence of worlds such as our own, in which under favourable conditions of temperature an eon-long evolutionary process can unroll itself, is a good deal rarer among the galaxies than was at one time supposed. Life and Man, without being unique, therefore, may be cosmically quite remarkable.

Since the guiding thread of rise of organization shows itself throughout the evolutionary process, we are to look for it in the history of human society as well. Only in the light of this can we assess the controversies between historians concerning progress in human history. The development of social organizations thus becomes obvious, and our duty in our own time is to ally ourselves with the forces of this saecular trend, since though the ultimate answer is not in doubt, the time of its arrival depends upon us.

No doubt the greatest effect of modern science on human civilization has been to unify the whole world's surface. Among the tasks of integration which humanity is now facing in the progress towards higher forms of order and union, none can well be thought larger than the confluence of the Euro-American and Chinese civilizations. The more one studies the two, the more do they seem, I feel, like two different symphonies by two different composers using identical fundamental melodies.

If modern science originated and developed wholly in the

West, it was due very largely to the existence of favourable social and economic conditions there, conditions which did not exist in China. Conditions in China were, indeed, definitely inhibitory to the growth of modern science and its associated technologies. But now for many years since the impact of Western civilization through the Chinese eastern coast, China has exerted herself to catch up with these developments, and today, of course, there are a large number of first-rate Chinese scientists and technologists in all fields.

If our personal duty in our day and age is to ally ourselves with all such forces as we may find at work in the world making towards higher levels of social integration, this generally means political action of one kind or another. One of its forms today is the promotion of all possible machinery of international co-operation.

Scientific humanism is at least as old as the pre-Socratic philosophers in Greece and the Chinese philosophers of the time of the Warring States in China. But its universal triumphs were reserved for the last few centuries, and its greatest are yet to come.

4

***

A POEM IN HIS OWN STYLE
(*for Rewi Alley*)

1945, first printed in *Science Outpost*, 1948

On the road to Chhang-an, making for Swordgate Pass,
At the end of August, through torrents of rain,
We came down to the water meadows by the flooding Fou-Chiang
Negotiating a subsidence, a culvert falling in,
And spent the night in a thatched hut, waiting for the crossing.
In the morning the river had swollen enormously
And was carrying away houses with thuds like the bombs of the Sung.

We retreated rapidly to higher ground,
But the culvert had fallen in further and our truck could not go back.
It was at the mercy of the waters until they should recede.
So there we were (the Greeks) trapped.

In an airy loft of a school we found temporary shelter
Drying our clothes, drying matches and books,
While the flood reached the level of our engine at its highest
And on every road bridges and telegraph lines were out.
So there we were, trapped (as Romans have been before).

But tasting the idea in one's mind
It did not seem so bad as might have been expected.

The seven-foot high white grasses look like spears
Hosting with the wind against the enemies of the Han
When you see them from a distance,
Or terrible as an army with banners;
But when, walking, you brush against them
They are soft and intimate, soft as the sleeve,
Soft as the footstep, of the Emperor's lovely one,
Restored to him, grieving, for an instant, by the art of Li Shao- hün.

A POEM IN HIS OWN STYLE (FOR REWI ALLEY)

There are moments of uncouthness
Moments also of unthinking loutish laughter,
Scowls on the faces of merchants and officials,
Squalor in the houses of the uninstructed—
But there was the little angel, in the thatched hut, with the blue trousers
    and the silver hair ornaments
There was the wife of Farmer Chou who roasted corncobs for us
There was the warm little room with the charcoal cooking-stove, and
    what Su-Hsüan's hands did.
There was the gay smile, more than mortal, of the boat boy gazing under
    his large hat at the river
(So Michael must have looked, facing the prince of chaos)
There was the *lao hsiang*, grave, wrinkled, benign:
'I remember no such floods since Kuang-Hsü, the sixteenth year'.
There were the two old Taoists at the pagoda temple
Moulding clay peaches in the luminous evening,
There was the gaitered geologist riding over the hills.

So many people, and eight out of ten, how could one help loving?
Was it trapped? Or rather, welcomed for a longer stay?
(Quaere:
An vir civilisationem sicut mulierum diligere possit?)
And if the stay should be indeed a long one,
If (like George) one should leave one's body in the red or the yellow earth
Or under the rocks ringing with the stone-hammers
Or beside the rhythmic chanting of the river
Or among the pines by the mountain road,
After all, one has to come to an end some time some where
An end of doing what one can to help.

And who needs help more than the black-haired people
Whom history did not favour?
Have they not suffered already far too long
For lack of the iron wheel, hard glass and yellow-green syrup
The tamed skyspark and the tethered thunderball?
The people who look as human beings ought to look
Blue-black hair, gold-brown skin, eyes like brown pools,
Beautiful thighs and noses not greedy,
But doomed to hard lives
Cramping diseases, and years barely threescore.
Sir Thomas was at home under any meridian
Mark of Genoa thought Hangchow the better,

Good people to help
A good place to lie.
There would be many works undone, of course,
But Heaven may know of a better instrument.

After ten days we were going on our way.
Mr. Wang, the highway engineer,
Poising his chopsticks, inviting to eat, said, 'I am afraid,
Our Chinese roads are really very bad.'
We (the Hellenes) replied, 'Not at all, they may do with some improve-
ment
But the Chinese weather is certainly sometimes rather severe.'

Lao hsiang: old countryman.

5

THE WAYS OF SZECHUAN

First published in *Asian Horizon*, 1948

Knowing the Cambridgeshire drifts and the Cotswold lanes
The lines of poplars in the Ile de France
The dusty roads where the country people of Lowicz
Go with the white kerchiefs and the rainbow skirts—
All are good;
But between dreaming and waking
It is always the pathways of Szechuan
One longs to tread again,
The steps of ancient stone ascending and descending
Winding through the rice-fields like bronze mirrors
Through the green explosions of bamboo thickets
Through the pines and through the drifting clouds.

Down to the ferry, the *ma-thou*,
Where the stone Omitofu grins at the rippling water
Frightening ghosts away;
Down to the swirling yellow Yangtze
Where naked boys dive from sun-bleached sampans
Where the songs of the pullers strain against the rocks
Where the salt-boats pass in silence downstream
Save for the sucking and swishing of little whirlpools
The rowers standing as in ancient Egypt
With Master Wu hanging over the steering-oar
And Lao Wang setting the rice to steam
(I can see it as if I were there).

Or up to the hermitage of Su Tung-Po
Past the cave-inscriptions and the colossal Boddhisattva
Where forestry experts examine their samples of wood
The wealth which has never known the ice;
Or up to the clouds and images of Chin-Yün Ssu

And the mild abbot brewing his peculiar tea;
Up to the agricultural experiment farm
With talk of phosphorus and nitrogen to and fro;
Up to the Alchemy Tower at Loukuantai
Where the Thang Taoists made their potable gold
(I can see it as if I were there).

And so often the rain
Dripping and dripping
From the lovely tiles to the runnels of stone
In the interior court
(Whoever would have expected to be homesick for rain?)
Its breath coming in through the broken paper window-panes
Living, in fact, with the weather,
Blowing at the hot tea,
Gossiping with friends,
May help in understanding the Tao.

Or else the sun
Fiercely arising
(Who dresses in comfort gets up before five)
Beating down on the farmers in the corn
On the hauliers on the long roads
Beautiful ones, old and young,
Earning a wretched living by expense of sweat
Resting perhaps at a turn in the path
Taking a puff from the belt's pipe and pouch
Under a spreading tree, beside a Thu-ti Miao,
Where the celestial mandarin, the genius of the place,
Keeps his long watch.

Up and Down, Water and Fire,
Yin and Yang, therefore, as it always was,
The Tao's Ministers of Left and Right,
Officials of the Order of Nature,
Ordering all coming-into-being and all passing-away,
Marshalling the distant clouds on summer evenings
Lit from within by lightning flashing,
Ordering the patience of the water-buffalo,
The ripening of oranges, and of lovers,
In their long blue gowns, in the twilight by the river—
'The Way that can be talked about is not the Eternal Way.'

The Ways of Szechuan

This is, of course, the Way of the Hsien, the True Ones,
But as to the Ways of wayfaring men,
Though everywhere under Heaven doubtless beautiful,
If you have known the Land of the Four Rivers
If you have journeyed on the steps of ancient stone
Ascending and descending, winding through the rice-fields
Through the pines and through the drifting clouds
That is what you see
Between sleeping and waking
And there you know you must return.

Ma-thou: ferry.
Omitofu: Buddhist image.
Thu-ti Miao: shrine of the tutelary deity.

6

THE 2500TH BIRTHDAY OF CONFUCIUS

THE RENEWED IMPORTANCE OF CHINESE THOUGHT

1951

In 549 B.C. there occurred the event which all Chinese are now celebrating, namely the birth of Confucius. Khung was his family name; his given name was Chhiu and his style Chung-Ni, but he is always referred to by his title of honour, Khung Tzu or Khung Fu-Tzu, that is Master Khung, whence the Latinized form Confucius. His family traced descent from the ancient dynastic house of Shang through the feudal family of Sung. He entered government service first as an official in charge of a city, Chung-tu. For a short time from 501 B.C. he was Deputy Minister of Justice and Chancellor of Protocol in the State of Lu (modern Shantung), but soon had to resign (497 B.C.), and for most of the rest of his life wandered in enforced exile from state to state seeking opportunity to employ his great talents but never finding it. The later years were spent in writing and the instruction of his disciples; he died in 479 B.C. Although his life might at the time have seemed something of a failure, his subsequent influence was so far-reaching as to justify the title often given to him of the 'uncrowned emperor' of China.

Modern research, though doubting the literary work traditionally attributed to Confucius, has thrown much light on two turning-points in his career. The first was when he successfully saved his prince by clever diplomacy from an ambush of ritual Pyrrhic dancers at an interview with the prince of Chhi. The second was when he tried to arrange for the dismantling of the Lu city-castles in order to restore authority to the prince and to reduce the power of the high feudal nobles. Their enmity pursued him long afterwards and accounts for the long period of his exile (till 484 B.C.).

For a time it seemed that his doctrines would fail to take root. The tyrannical authoritarianism and draconic laws of the Legalist School, widely adopted, permitted the ruler of the State of Chhin to unify the whole empire and to become its first emperor; but they brought their own inevitable downfall and within fifty years the long-lived dynasty of the Han had come to power. Confucianism then showed itself to be the most suitable system of thought for the growth of that bureaucratism which was to be the characteristic social system of China, and the Legalists, together with the remaining philosophical schools (with the notable exception of the Taoists) descended into that perennial darkness from which only modern scholarship has resurrected them.

Confucianism was a deeply humanitarian paternalistic ethic cast in the mould of the feudal society in which it was born. It was passionately devoted to social justice, in so far as that could be conceived in feudal, and later in feudal-bureaucratic, society. It embodied a sceptical rationalism which had echoes throughout Chinese history, and which would have been very favourable to the development of modern science if its effect had not been overweighted by the intensive concentration of Confucian interest on human society and human society alone. If bureaucratism, in suppressing the rise of the merchants as a group to a position of power in the body politic, sterilized that very social class which was in European history so closely bound up with the rise of modern science and technology, that was not the fault of Confucianism as a philosophy. But Confucianism mirrored in the world of the mind the actual conditions of Chinese medieval social life, in which all intermediate feudal lords had disappeared, and the imperial house collected its taxes by means of a bureaucracy of scholars so gigantic and so influential as to have no counterpart in European history.

If Confucianism was the doctrine of the scholar when in office, Taoism, as has often been said, was the doctrine of the scholar when out of office, or of the scholar who would not accept office.

Taoist thought was in all respects the contrary of Confucian. The Taoists were deeply interested in Nature (the word Tao as used by them may perhaps best be translated the Order of Nature), and they felt, in their bones, as we say, that until man understood more about the great world in which he found himself, human society would never be properly governable. If the Confucians paralleled the Stoics of our own antiquity, the Taoists paralleled the Atomists and Epicureans. Taoism has been described by the eminent Chinese philosopher Fêng Yu-Lan as 'the only system of mysticism which the world has ever seen which was not profoundly anti-scientific'. And in truth it turned out that all the Chinese sciences and technologies grew up with Taoist affiliations; the Taoist search for the drug of immortality gave rise to alchemy, probably older in China than anywhere else, and to botany and pharmaceutics; the ironworkers and salt-miners, the men who invented the first efficient animal harness and the earliest deep drilling, all venerated Taoist genii. Confucian masculine managing social aggressiveness was matched throughout the centuries by Taoist feminine receptive individualist withdrawal, as if the Yang and the Yin were two inescapable moulds of human personality.

Buddhism stood outside this world. It was to China as much a foreign religion as Manichaeism or Christianity, and although it had brilliant successes there, embedding itself deeply in folklore and manners of thought, it has never lost the stamp of its foreign origin. Most observers of Chinese life in recent years (and I agree with them) consider that the influence of Buddhism is greatly on the decline, while on the other hand the basic ideas of Confucianism and of Taoism are the universal mental background of every Chinese, no matter how cosmopolitan education or circumstances may have made him. Of course Confucianism as an apologetic for persisting 'feudal' social relations, and Taoism as an escapist and superstitious religion, will be attacked by the progressive forces now at work. But many of the best elements of Chinese life derive from these two systems of thought. Is it not therefore important that they should now receive a renewed examination by the rest of the world?

Today we are facing the fact that 700 million people, belonging to one of the most ancient and beautiful cultures of humanity, which has influenced the civilization of the Occident far more than is generally recognized, are incorporating themselves in the 'Left Half of the World'. Those who knew China during the late war have not been much surprised at the course which events have taken. The 'scholar-gentry' ruled China with considerable success for two thousand years, but for adequate modernization and participation in the unified world of modern technology a profound metamorphosis was necessary. Sun Yat-Sen began it and it is still taking place. What will be the effect upon the world of these changes?

In the eighteenth century the Encyclopaedists, who carefully studied the Latin translations of the Chinese classics made by the Jesuits, discovered that for centuries Confucianism had inculcated a morality without supernaturalism, and that the Pelagian doctrine of the intrinsic goodness of human nature (essential for any progressive social philosophy) had been orthodox, not heretical, in China. Such discoveries prepared the way for the French revolution. Is it not possible, therefore, that, given time, the philosophical background of so vast a population and so deep-rooted a culture, may exert similar stimulating effects upon the development of collectivist thought, and even do something towards drawing the two halves of the world together?

If anything of this kind should occur, it would not be likely to be in the domain of the Marxist economic analysis, or fundamental doctrines such as the ownership of the means of production by the people as a whole. There is no reason to think that the Chinese will not make as convinced socialists as anybody else. But there are certain directions in which Chinese thinking might have a profound effect upon the nature of the society of the future, perhaps in the matter of the juristic security of the individual, and in the forms which the numinous will take in that society.

Those who have criticized the U.S.S.R. for the lack of individual juristic security which has existed there, have often overlooked the facts, not only that the Russian themselves have desired a higher measure of it but have considered themselves prevented by the persistence of what they feel to be a state of hostility (even if only of the 'cold' variety); but also that Russian conceptions derive inevitably, through Eastern Orthodoxy, from Byzantine autocracy, and not from Roman law. Since the countries of western Europe have been drawn, on account of the similarity of their parliamentary institutions, into the domain of the 'Right Half of the World', it may be difficult for their traditions to affect the traditions of collectivist society for some considerable time to come. But this will not be the case for Chinese traditions, which will henceforth be fully available to stimulate the thinking of the collectivist countries. The popular idea that Chinese law and penal practice were always very backward is a purely nineteenth-century misconception; on the contrary, the early Portuguese travellers in the sixteenth century constantly drew attention to what they considered the much greater humanity of Chinese magistrates and legal procedure as compared with contemporary Europe, especially as regards the value placed on the individual and the value of negotiated compromise solutions. And many of the Jesuits thought the same. Hence it is clear that Chinese conceptions of law and justice call urgently for more careful study.

So also for the manifestations which the numinous may take in the society of the future. The sense of the holy can nowhere more markedly be found than in Confucian temples, yet the Master never spoke about the 'gods and spirits', had no cosmology, still less any theology, and if himself later 'deified', was only so treated in the complimentary, courteous, and largely poetic way which the Chinese have of dealing with notable inventors, virtuous governors, and particularly beneficent dragons. The Master said: 'If the world was as it ought to be, I should not be wanting to change it.' In erecting the Mausoleum of Lenin outside the Kremlin wall, the Russians were, no doubt unconsciously, adopting a practice which the Chinese had known for thousands of years before. There may thus be some analogy between the Kremlin tomb and the age-old temple of the Sage in Shantung, which many from all countries in the world had hoped to be able to visit in this anniversary year.

There seems recently to have been a growing tendency among the leaders of the Christian Churches to align themselves with the less conciliatory elements in the 'Right Half of the World.' If this continues they will lose all chance of embodying the influence of Christian ideas in future collectivist societies. But on his 2500th birthday, fields of influence hitherto undreamed of seem to be opening before Master Khung of the State of Lu.

7

THE CONFUCIAN TEMPLE
AT CHHANG-AN
1964

The Confucian Temple at Chhang-an, modern Sian in Shensi, is one of the most beautiful in China, and contains in its grounds the Pei Lin or 'Forest of Steles', the greatest extant collection of ancient and mediaeval Chinese inscribed monuments.

At the age of forty-four my steps first led me here,
In a time of oppression by landlords and foreign troops.
Thick grass and thistles surrounded the lovely halls
Floating like ships in a sea of jungle green.
The wooden brackets were sagging, the terrace balconies broken,
And ordure of occupation intruded on the fragrance of the Sage.
The stone steles of the ancients seemed truly like forest trees
Springing from the undergrowth of wasteland gone to seed.
Truly said Lao Tzu: 'Where an army has been it is thick with thorns.'
I bought Nestorian rubbings from a poverty-stricken shop,
I drank a cup of wine to the glory of past Chhang-an,
And mounting my decrepit ambulance with its grinding gears
Drove off over the Chhin-ling Shan to help in the anti-fascist war.

Fourteen years brought me again to the capital of Han,
No little thing had happened – a whole people had stood up.
Our Gerrard Winstanley had dreamed it on Cobham Hill:
'Ye Diggers all, stand up now, stand up!'; that was his song.
Right thinking, as Sakyamuni said, had led to right results
(Only it was not despair of the world, but just the opposite).
And thus I found all things ordered well, and the *phai-lou* erect,
And the gardens swept and garnished, and archaeology enthroned,
And learning honoured, as Confucius himself would have wished.

The Confucian Temple at Chhang-an

So I wrote in the book that the Stones had come to life again,
The Phoenix and the Unicorn had appeared once more in Chhang-an.
Words so warm that they moved a Far Westerner to quote them
(Though not without a scoff at their political faith).

At the age of sixty-four and with whitening hair
I return (may the Tao be praised) to this Literary Temple.
Having written much, whether well or ill I know not,
But with devout intention for the healing of the nations,
Shall I come again to Kuan-chung? Who can say?
The skies are serene, the sun hot in the Seric summer, but anxiety lingers,
Ever more dangerous grows the time – with forces abroad
That man may not have learnt to control; but with all Chinese friends
I hope, I hope, that Confucius' belief in man was the just one.
For all justice and righteousness, all learning and love,
We pray, we believe, that the peoples will bury the bomb and not otherwise.
And far in the future the sons of Kungshu Phan will bring other trials,
Many shall run to and fro and there will be many inventions
Testing man's body and soul to the point of destruction.
Then will be needed the last equilibrium, the ultimate krasis,
The perfect balance of Yin and Yang, the humanism of man,
The not too rational rationality, the not too irrational faith.
The world may be saved in that day by the Chinese tradition.
'At the root man's nature is fundamentally good.'
Ta Shêng Chung-Kuo! Jen Min Wên-Hua Wan Sui!
Let brotherhood cover the earth as the waters the sea.

Lao Tzu: the greatest Taoist sage, a semi-historical figure, the putative author of the greatest Taoist classic, the *Tao Tê Ching* (Canon of the Virtue of the Tao).
Phai-lou: triumphal gateway of wood or stone.
Tao: the Order of Nature.
Kuan-chung: 'the metropolitan region within the passes', i.e. the Wei River valley north of the Chhin-ling Mountains, in Shensi.
Kungshu Phan: fifth-century B.C. artisan and engineer of the State of Lu, afterwards patron saint of all technological men down through the ages.
Ta Shêng Chung-Kuo: 'Let the Chinese people loudly shout!'
Jen Min Wên-Hua Wan Sui: 'Long live the culture of the Chinese People!'

Confucian temples are called Wên Miao, i.e. literary temples, or temples of literary culture.

8

SAINTS IN CHINESE CULTURE

This review of *The Censorial System of Ming China* by C. O. Hucker, published by Stanford University Press in 1966, was first published in *Cambridge Review*, 1968

One of the greatest themes in the history of social institutions is the comparative study of administrative bureaucracies. Far from being of purely academic interest, nothing could be more vital for us today, since all societies on both sides of the more and more mythical 'iron curtain' are moving in the direction of more and more powerful bureaucracies. This trend is impossible to reverse. for it is necessitated by the very dependence of modern life on highly organized technology, but what everyone wants to know is how this unavoidable bureaucracy can be humanized and made to work in the interests of the people rather than those of particular influence groups or the apparatus itself. Socialist legality was not able to prevent the horrifying oppression of the Stalin period, which had not the justification of the built-in anti-morality and the racial diabolism of the Nazi–Fascist states, but in lesser degree the powers of government are often felt to be oppressive in the capitalist democracies, as witness the American withdrawal of citizens' passports, or such cases as the Stansted dispute in the United Kingdom. The ombudsman system of the Scandinavians has been one attempt to answer this problem, but it is far from solved, and probably no tag is destined to be more long-lived than Acton's 'all power corrupts, and absolute power corrupts absolutely'. Why not have a look, therefore, at the structure of the world's oldest bureaucracy, that of traditional China, to see if any 'checks and balances' were built into that system, so extraordinarily successful that it lasted well over two thousand years, and still lives on in transmuted form in the People's Republic of the present day?

Hence the interest of the book here reviewed, far greater than that of a monograph only suitable for sinologists' shelves. Professor Charles Hucker, one of our soundest Chinese social historians, has chosen to examine in great detail the working of the *Censoriat* during two periods of the Ming dynasty in the fifteenth and seventeenth centuries A.D. For indeed there existed in the Chinese bureaucratic system from the Han period onward a system of control which involved a quasi-independent supervision of the officials on the one hand and a quasi-independent criticism of the emperor on the other. As soon as the first unification of the empire had taken place, in the third century B.C., government function naturally generated two chains of command, that of the civil executive under the 'prime minister' (*tshai-hsiang*) and that of the military forces under the 'grand marshal' (*ta-ssuma*). What was much more remarkable was that by the Han three organs of government developed equal in rank, the executive secretariat and magisteriat (provincial and city governors, directors of special services, counsellors and the like), the military commissariat (generals, officers, strategists and the like), and the censoriat (*yü-shih thai*) under the Censor-in-chief (*yü-shih ta-fu*). Later on this again developed into two pyramids of officials, the surveillance officials or Inspectors (*chha kuan*) and the speaking officials or Remonstrators (*yen kuan*). The former were in principle charged with investigating the activities of all members of the executive branch whether in the capital or the provinces, and impeaching any whom they believed guilty of malpractices; the latter were charged with the opposite duty of scrutinizing all imperial edicts and actions, and remonstrating with the emperor if any of these were felt to be contrary to the ideals of the Confucian ethico-philosophical system. The censors did not, Hucker writes in his conclusion, 'characteristically serve as agents of imperial oppression and terrorization of the people and the

H

officialdom, nor did they characteristically serve as agents of popular or bureaucratic resistance to imperial domination. Most characteristically they were spokesmen for and defenders of a traditionalism to which the emperors, the officialdom and the people at large were equally committed and which no one seriously challenged. In this capacity they cautioned and harassed emperors and officials alike, and within the limits imposed by the power structure and the ideology to which they were wed, they could and did mitigate oppression, injustice and malfeasance, sometimes at great cost to themselves.'

The institution of the censoriat deeply impressed Western observers from Ricci and Trigault around 1610 through Semedo in 1655 to Wells Williams in 1883. In our own time it has been the subject of undue praise by Lin Yü-Thang and ludicrous denigration by Wittfogel. Contrary to the implications of the former it cannot be seen as the mouthpiece of popular opinion; the censors were never remotely like political revolutionaries. Contrary to the statements of the latter it cannot be seen as an instrument of despotic oppression like some sort of secret police; the censors were never the tools of the emperor in his dealings with his officials. 'Neither representatives of the imperial will,' says Hucker, 'nor representatives of the majority will, they were spokesmen of the general will – that is to say, guardians of the Confucian governmental heritage handed down from the past.' Even in terms of Marxist sociology, for which the entire bureaucratic superstructure was the characteristic form of exploitation of men within the 'Asiatic mode of production', the censoriat was one essential component of the machine which made its working tolerable and assured its millennial continuance. The autonomous censoriat had direct access to the throne, so much so that censors of all subordinate ranks could memorialize directly without authorization from their chiefs, they were normally of low rank and relatively young (for very good reasons), and they had the right of inquisition (if the term is not misplaced) into all persons and all government accounts and documents. This remarkable system, the creation of Chinese genius, is not of course absolutely without historical parallels in Europe. Hucker mentions the ephors of ancient Sparta, the *missi dominici* of Charlemagne, the fiscals of Frederick the Great and Peter the Great, the inspectors-general of Napoleon, etc., and one could easily add other examples, for example, the Inquisitor sent by the Pope to Malta in 1572 to be a permanent thorn in the flesh of the Bishop at Mdina no less than the Grand Masters of the Knights of St. John at Valletta. But none of these had anything like the scale and scope of the Chinese censoriat. The really important questions are whether the Soviet Union could have gone so far off the rails in the Stalinist period if something like the censoriat had been built into its governmental structure, whether a religion or a social philosophy with strongly numinous overtones such as Confucianism is or is not a necessary condition for the operation of such a device, and whether for the bureaucratic societies of the future, all likely to be broadly socialist in nature, something deeply valuable could not be learnt from the built-in Chinese control system.

Exactly how well the censoriat worked as a piece of machinery at different times is a separate question. Hucker tests it analytically for the periods 1424–34 and 1620–27. The first of these was a relatively tranquil time, the second disturbed even to chaos by the impending invasion of the Manchu people. In the former the censoriat was active in carrying out its prescribed duties, and the emperors generally approved both the impeachments and the advice of its members, each month bringing one or two major démarches of each kind. In the latter, conditions were very different; the emperor was generally at odds with the censors, whose impeachment initiatives ran as high as six a month, and proposals and remonstrances as high as fifteen every month. What was much worse, the censoriat failed to prevent the rise to power of the tyrannical eunuch Wei Chung-Hsien, characteristic of the period, and was presently packed with his nominees; after which they harassed military commanders in the field so severely as to contribute a good deal to the defeat of the Chinese by the Manchus, and effectively prevented some of the Grand Secretaries from performing their duties. The fault was in the system, which pre-supposed a firm imperial hand at the helm; and as this was lacking, the censoriat merely contributed to chaos and stagnation. Many another detailed study will be needed before we have a clear picture of the functioning of the censoriat in different periods and different dynasties, but this should give us much information far more than purely historical in value.

For one thing it ought to contribute to the better understanding of a non-Christian civilization by Europeans grounded in Christendom. Their clear need today is to find in the non-European civilizations manifestations of those values to which they themselves feel so deeply committed, not to attempt, as formerly they did, to mould all other cultures into their own image. If therefore anyone should be looking for saints in Chinese culture, could they not be found in those learned and virtuous members of the censoriat who generation after generation rose to rebuke vice and injustice, even at the risk of their lives and liberties, sometimes being mown down one after another, yet persisting in their stand on behalf of the traditions of Confucian morality? Martyrs there often were, as Hucker's book in more than one place touchingly relates, and these are the men whom Europeans should, though belatedly, learn to know and to venerate.

9

THE BALLAD OF MÊNG CHIANG NÜ
WEEPING AT THE GREAT WALL

Translation from a traditional broadsheet
bought at the Temple of the City-God at
Lanchow, 1943; first published in *Sinologica* (with Liao Hung-Ying), 1948

The ballad goes:—

(*Buddhist introductory verse; seven-character lines*)

Spring, summer, autumn, winter, deep cold and summer heat, pass by,
Suns and moons together revolving purify the heart in the end,
A little while on earth, those who do good deeds,
Will reach at last the Western Heaven founded of old.

(*Taoist introduction; in prose*)

   In the province of Chhinchow [Thienshui in modern Kansu province,] in
the *hsien* city of Chiangni, in the Fan village [of the clan Fan], there was a local
Yuan-Wai official who often fasted and did many good deeds. He had no son.
He and his wife fasted and gave alms for three years, and at last she bore a
wonderful baby whose name was Mêng Chiang. To such good people the girl
was a gift from Heaven. The Jade Emperor came down from his throne and
the girl came down to earth. She had to suffer from evil spirits in order to be a
lesson to ordinary people. Afterwards she married Fan San-Lang, who was
himself a golden child come down from Heaven.

(*Buddhist interpolation; still prose but in groups of seven characters*)

In a world of plants: the rice comes first
In a world full of dishes : the prince can eat everywhere
Yellow gold and white jade : are truly valueless
To put on monks' robes : is the most difficult thing
Once the great King : of the mountains and rivers
Grieving for country and commons, said : 'My work ever increasing

117

A hundred years : and thirty-six thousand days
Do not equal a half day's leisure : of the Buddhist monk.
My regrets circle always : round one mistake
Not to have changed the imperial yellow : for the Buddhist purple
Originally I was : a poor boy in the west
How did I come to fall : into an Imperial House?
Jade Girls and Golden Boys : descend to the earth
The wheels of birth and death : number thousands upon thousands
The erring people : do not at all repent
The worldly care nothing : for the actions of the just,
In the three hells : their suffering will be unbearable
One day the unusual happens : and in an instant all is over
Even a man's own bedding : will quickly disappear
All these worldly riches : avail nought in the end
Your well-loved children : and wives cannot come to you
In your familiar places : no one will know you more
But bodily discipline and purity of mind : brings happiness without sorrow.'

(The ballad proper; seven-character lines, we use William Langland's metre)

  1. Now about good people : and their way
     Where they come from : how should I know?
     There was a man of the name of Hsü : whose title was Yuan-Wai
     He lived with his family : in the city of Chiangni

  2. He fasted and did : many good deeds
     No sons had he : but a beautiful daughter
     When one month old : she was brought forth to be named
     To go through the ceremony : of godmother-giving

  3. Her father's name Hsü : her mother's name Mêng
     Her godmother's name Chiang : so did it chance
     Thus she was called : Mêng Chiang Nü
     All wished her long life : happiness and honour

  4. In the first and second years : her mother carried her in arms
     In the third and fourth : she did not leave her mother's side
     In the fifth and sixth : they bound her feet
     In the seventh and eighth : she embroidered mandarin-ducks

  5. In the sixteenth year : her body's growth was accomplished
     Her father engaged her : to the gentle youth Fan San-Lang
     At sixteen he had achieved : the first scholar's degree
     So then he took : the girl to wife

6. She combed her hair : and said goodbye to her ancestors
   With tears rushing down : she honoured her parents' high hall
   Her husband's people : quickly had come
   With flowery flags and feasting : with a chair of dignity and light

7. The chair followed the old : Chou Kung customs
   She worshipped Heaven and Earth : and bowed low to her parents
   United into one : the two entered the bridechamber
   And she lived right happily : with husband and mother-in-law

8. Half a month had hardly gone : before the tyrant Emperor
   Chhin Shih Huang Ti : began to build the Great Wall
   Her husband's name was pricked : so he took in his hands
   The carrying-pole : and the ropes and baskets

9. Thus husband and wife : were torn apart and scattered
   The mandarin-ducks : separated and sundered
   He spoke sorrowful words : making ready to go
   While Mêng Chiang Nü : watched him from the gate

10. He turned his head : looking back longingly
    Lingering loth to leave : little Mêng Chiang Nü
    'I am now departing : to work at the Great Wall
    You in the family : must wait upon the old ones

11. In order that we may : meet again hereafter
    We must wait till the Wall : is successfully completed.'
    The which having said : he set off on his way
    Leaving Mêng Chiang Nü behind : full of tears

12. Now we will not rede : of what her husband did
    But we will speak of the skirt : and the silver hair-ornaments
    In the first and second months : he did not return
    In the third and fourth : she did not see him

13. In the fifth and sixth : the heat was difficult to bear –
    In the seventh and eighth : the autumn wind was cold
    In the ninth and tenth : there was still no news
    When the winter really came : the frosts were terrible

14. Every family was making : well-padded clothes
    And sending them to those : who had gone to build the Wall
    Mêng Chiang Nü made some : thinking of him
    The pain shot through : her liver and kidneys

15. You have no brothers : she thought to herself
    Who now will boldly bring you : such warm clothes
    Others have elder : and younger brothers
    To bear to the border baillies : winter protection

16. Thus saying she went weeping : to her tapestried chamber
    Lay on her bed : and thought about him
    Never has there been : news of him nor tidings
    Deserted and dolorous : I bide day and night

17. I speak not of the first and second : night-watch bamboo-strokes
    But it seemed not long after : I heard the third from the bridge-tower
    And then at midnight : upon the beats of the drum
    There came the spirit : of Fan San-Lang

18. Weeping, weeping : he entered the chamber
    Stooped over the bed : with tears falling
    'I am freezing to death' : he seemed to say
    'Quickly make for me : a padded gown

19. Separated am I : so far from the family
    The wicked king has sent me : to build the Great Wall
    Since boyhood by my books I bided : I have little brute strength
    How can I be expected : to do this cruel work?

20. Suddenly I felt faint : and fell to the ground
    Thus was I buried in the Wall : as it was a-building
    So tonight I your lover : come to make you this dream
    Neglect not my words : like wind passing in the air

21. Continue to be filial : to the old parents
    And fetch back the bones : and spirit of your husband
    In this life I shall not now : be able to return so far
    But in our next rebirth : we shall surely meet again

22. Many and many things, girl : I have to tell you of –'
    But the cock crowed : compelling the spirit to vanish
    Reluctant to leave its love : it went out of the gate
    Withdrew to the Great Wall : and waited for the padded gown

23. Mêng Chiang Nü was very frightened : and looked all around
    But could not see her love : anywhere near
    She sat on the bed : and thought on what had happened
    Was it a dream : or was it not?

24. Whatever it was : it filled me with sorrow
    He said he had met : danger while working
    Was like to be killed : and buried within the Wall
    His body all shivering : with cold and frost

25. He asked me to send clothes : and move his spirit
    To look after the old hall : with piety and reverence
    And to guard my widowhood : truly and faithfully
    And he said we should some day : be united again

26. How could it be : but an empty dream?
    So turning to left : and right in her sorrow
    She could not help tears : flooding out in the night
    And so continued : until the dawn

27. Mêng Chiang Nü got up : and put on her clothes
    Combed her hair : made toilet and habit
    Quickly she went then : into the kitchen place
    Prepared tea and rice : for the old people

28. Then going into : the tapestried chamber
    She gave them to know : what the words
    And what the happenings : in the dark night
    'Your daughter-in-law : must to the border pass. ·

29. She wishes to deliver : clothes to your son'
    Then the two old people : rose up affrighted
    'Good daughter-in-law : do not be in such haste
    The frontier is so far : distant from here

30. Who will escort you : at your forth faring?
    Good daughter-in-law : you are but a woman
    How can you travel : alone and unattended?
    You should stay at home : and minister to us

31. If you wait till our son : comes back to this countryside
    Mother and son, man and wife : all then will be happy.'
    Hearing these words : Mêng Chiang Nü wept again
    'You two old people : listen to my counsel

32. Others have elder brothers : others have younger
    Who can go to the border pass : to take warm clothes
    None such truly : has your son
    How shall he get : the clothing he needs?

33. Himself he came to me : in the dark night
    And begged your daughter-in-law : for a padded gown
    Now is my mind : firmly determined
    I must go to the border pass : to search for San-Lang

34. If I am able : there to see his face
    We will both return : to the family and countryside
    We shall gather in the high hall : and wait upon you merrily
    But if it be : that his face I see not

35. I shall die in the wilderness : and not return home.'
    This being said : she went to a small room
    And busily opened : a gilded box
    Took out a few : warm padded garments

36. Took out leggings and shoes : pairs two or three
    Rolled them all up : in a bundle burden
    Shouldered it quickly : took all else needful
    Said farewell to the parents : and went on her way

37. Very desolate and sad : were the two old people
    But we will say no more : of them and their sorrow
    We shall rede rather : of the virtuous wife
    Mêng Chiang Nü : in the midst of the way

38. Inly she revolved : how hard her journey
    How to reach the borderlands : she did not know
    Pondering in what direction : the Great Wall might be
    Weeping she walked : and wended her way

39. Would that by a single step : she could attain her goal
    Mind mazed, step speedy : heart burning, head heavy
    Her heart full of flowers : she fell down at a certain spot
    Near where Kuan Yin the great Goddess : was sitting on a lotus

40. Whose ears grew hot : her eyes swelled in her head
    Her mind was perturbed : 'What now do I see?
    It is the virtuous wife : Mêng Chiang Nü in anguish
    Was she not once a Jade Girl : in the heavens above?

41. Consort of the Golden Boy : Fan San-Lang?
    Now in the midst of the road : in such great trouble
    Taking clothes to her husband : a thousand miles
    If I do not save her : what power will do so?

42. Right soon shall I save : Mêng Chiang Nü.'
    She opened her mouth : and called to her attendants
    'Go to the road : and attend upon the girl.'
    Immediately they obeyed : her holy wish

43. In a flash they arrived : at the place on the road
    Lifted her up : far above the clouds
    To deliver her straightway : at the Great Wall
    With one single cloud : she sailed three thousand *li*

44. Fast and furious : beyond her control
    Fast and furious : ascending and descending
    She reached the Great Wall : at noontide was it
    Then the cloud clearing : she looked down

45. There was the Great Wall : mountains and moorlands
    And there she was set down : and felt again the solid earth
    On which she had been born : while the attendants returned
    To the heavenly palace : and reported to the Goddess

46. Suddenly she opened her eyes : and wept with amaze
    To see the Great Wall : extended before her
    The width of the Wall : was several times ten feet
    To east and west : you could never see the end of it

47. In her mind she wondered : where he could be
    And how she could have reached : this waste so weird
    Wide have I been wafted : by some holy spirits
    And so brought : to the Great Wall

48. Immediately she knelt : on the ground gratefully
    Giving grace to the company of the Gods : and thanking high Heaven
    So bowing she rose : and straightway began
    • Her search for her husband : along the Great Wall

49. While she was awalking : she lifted up her head and looked
    And saw a field full of folk : building at the Wall
    Approaching them fearfully : she opened her mouth and asked
    'You big brothers : please lend me your ears

50. There was a man : from the town of Chiangni
    Fan San-Lang : was his earthly name
    He was only aged : seventeen or eighteen
    Where can I find him : at work on the Wall?

51. Big brothers : please tell me if you know?
    I am his wife : Mêng Chiang Nü
    Thousands of *li* I have come : bringing padded clothes
    But as yet I have not seen : where he is.'

52. They heard her words : and their hearts were moved
    They thought of their own families : and their own parents
    And they too had brothers : big and small
    Whom as yet they had not seen : coming with clothes

53. They thought too of their own : dear wives and lemans
    Good, but not so good : as the virtuous Mêng Chiang
    So they answered and said : to Mêng Chiang Nü
    'Good sister-in-law : you listen to our story

54. About this man : from the town of Chiangni
    Whose name we understand : was Fan San-Lang
    Whose age was only : seventeen or eighteen
    Surely he was in Tungkung : building the Wall

55. Every man suffered there : a thousand hardships
    And we heard he died : by the Great Wall in that place
    Good sister-in-law : if more you would know
    Follow along the Wall : and enquire of our mates.'

56. Mêng Chiang Nü : heard what they said
    Could not help shedding : bitter tears once again
    Then suddenly fainted : before them all
    Her three *hun* essences : visited the world above

57. And her seven *pho* essences : the home of the dead
    Though the Underworld King : controls the affairs of souls
    He has little power over those : of people still living
    So they were able : to wander for a while at will

58. Coming to herself : she uttered such a cry
    That the Jade Emperor in his palace above : was alarmingly stirred
    Seated on his throne : his ears grew hot
    His eyes swelled in his head : and his mind was perturbed

59. He shouted for his assistant : who can see a thousand *li*
    'Below there on earth : who suffers so unjustly?'
    The company of the gods : immediately replied
    'Your majesty, please listen : to what we have to tell

60. On earth below : from the town of Chiangni
    A young conscript was taken : Fan San-Lang his name
    He was in the beginning : a Golden Boy in heaven
    And his wife Mêng Chiang Nü : a Jade Girl also

61. At the Great Wall : he met with danger
    So that his bones and body : are buried therein
    Mêng Chiang Nü has come : thousands of *li* with clothes
    And now she is crying herself to death : at the Great Wall.'

62. Then the Jade Emperor : in a passion flew
    On account of this Jade Girl : this suffering star
    From Ling-Hsiao Tien pavilion : orders instantly went out
    Summoning the Dragon Prince : and all the company of the Gods

63. The Thunder Duke and the Lightning Mother : appeared as commanded
    'You heavenly spirits : pay heed now to my words
    The place where Fan San-Lang : was building the Wall
    Now contains : his bones and his body

64. You must find them and hand them : to Mêng Chiang Nü
    To take back a thousand *li* : to family and countryside.'
    Thus the company of the gods : received the jade orders
    With good omens and clouds like drapery : they descended from
        heaven's courts

65. Soon they reached the Great Wall : in trampling and bustle
    Soon there sounded in the sky : a thunderous noise
    For the space of several *li* : the sides of the Wall were opened
    Exposing the white bones : of Fan San-Lang

66. Mêng Chiang Nü bending her head : looked at them closely
    Corpses and bones aglare : under the blue sky
    Mêng Chiang Nü : pondered in her heart
    Which of these could be : her husband's bones

67. Again she bent her head : and deeply thought
    What harm would it be : to bite the middle finger?
    If any bones be those : of her dear husband
    The fresh blood would certainly : soak and seep into them

68. But if they be not : truly his bones
    The blood would not enter : but run down to the ground
    So she then bit hard : upon the middle finger
    It bled fresh blood : streaming down in big drops

69. Immediately Mêng Chiang Nü : applied the test of blood
It soaked into the bones : showing they were her husband's
Mêng Chiang Nü was incredulous : still did she doubt
Why not apply the same : to some other bones also?

70. So this did she do : to seven or eight others
From all which the blood : ran straight down to the ground
Then Mêng Chiang Nü : felt an aching in her heart
Embracing the dead bones : she cried bitter tears

71. Wept that she could not : more see her husband
No more would they enter : together the bedchamber
'How pitiful, how pitiful : you that were a scholar
That the tyrant Emperor : should send you to build the Wall

72. You said you would return home : when the work was done
Who could foretell that at the Wall : you would visit the Yellow Springs
Think now of me : my love in the underworld
So that your bones : may safely be moved home.'

73. So saying she spread : wrappings on the ground
Lifted the bones tenderly : placed them inside
And made up a little parcel : tied with cords
With which she prepared : homeward to fare

74. Now hardly was she started : on her long journey
Than the wicked Chhin Shih Huang Ti : came by that way
With officials and soldiers : noble and numberless
With spears, pikes and swords : like a forest of hemp

75. With ladies of honour : and maidens in pairs
With canopies and fans : bright like the sun and moon
In the middle there stood : an imperial baldakin
Under which sat stately : the wicked Emperor

76. Mêng Chiang Nü terrified : dared not go near
She stood on the roadside : with tears streaming down
Till lifting up his head : the Emperor observed her
A woman of the commons : before him on the roadside

77. Perfect in beauty : was Mêng Chiang Nü
Than the spirit-girl Chiao Wo : much more excellent
Desire arose : in the Emperor's heart
And he ordered the court maids : to call the girl thither

126

78. The maids obeyed : no delay made they
    Coming to Mêng Chiang Nü : they asked her kindly
    'Whose woman are you : standing here?
    His Majesty calls on you : for an account.'

79. Mêng Chiang Nü : could not but approach
    Bowed and called out thrice : 'Long live the Enlightened One'
    Then the wicked Emperor : opened his mouth
    And ordered them all : to listen carefully

80. 'Where do you come from : you young woman?
    Clearly relate to me : your names and qualities
    I would know for what purpose : you have come here
    Plainly discover : your tale to the Lonely One.'

81. Having heard these questions : Mêng Chiang Nü answered
    'May it please your Majesty : listen from on high
    I live in a small town : called Chiangni
    Where the Fan family : is of good repute

82. Fan Yi-Shan : was the name of the father
    Who fasted daily : in front of the Buddha
    The mother, Li : repeated the Sutras
  ○ They took me, when orphaned : into their home

83. I, Mêng Chiang Nü : of the Hsü family
    Since childhood was engaged : to Fan San-Lang
    We did not expect : My Lord wanted to build the Wall
    And would conscript : the men of Chiangni

84. He being a scholar : lacked physical strength
    How could he do heavy work: fit for labourers?
    So he fainted : and fell to the ground
    And died and was buried : within the Great Wall

85. My husband's spirit : came back home
    Begged for warm clothes : from me, his wife,
    And asked if need be : to fetch his body home
    It shivered with cold : hunger and loneliness

86. I, your servant-maid : obeyed this vision
    So came I hither : to receive the bones
    And being duly protected : by the company of the gods
    Quickly I reached : the region of the Wall

87. Suddenly there sounded above : a thunderous noise
Which caused to tumble down : whole lengths of the Wall
By the power of the gods : revealing my husband's bones
Which I was able to identify : with the test of blood

88. These are the pains and sufferings : of Your Majesty's maid-servant
Is this sad, I ask : or is it not?'
The wicked Emperor : having listened to all
Said 'Maiden, now : may your heart be at peace

89. Your face seems to me : comely and beautiful
Follow the Lonely One to the court : and be made a Lady of Chao Yang
But should you disobey : my imperial words
How can you bear the crime : of Crying Down the Great Wall?'

90. The Emperor then : called up the axe-bearer
To be ready to strike off her head : there on the spot
Mêng Chiang Nü : hearing these words
Bent her head low : and considered carefully

91. By disobedience : I shall meet death
And leave my husband's body : in a strange place
Suddenly an idea : dawned there upon her
'Your Majesty, the Son of Heaven : is all-knowing

92. If I die now : I shall not be filial
Give me a hundred days : to carry out your order.'
Then the wicked Emperor : burst out laughing
And said 'Woman, be at ease : you shall not be harmed

93. Embroider a gown : for me, the Lonely One
And then you may return : home with the bones
Show me your gratitude : by your willingness
And afterwards I will let you go : freely with honour.'

(Interpolation concerning the gown; in ten-character lines)

You who wish to know about the removal of the body and the embroidery
of the gown, please listen to what follows:

Mêng Chiang Nü listened and wept, saying,
'Your Majesty orders me to embroider a gown to pardon my crime
Then pray quickly get people to spin the silk for me
I will embroider a gown of purple and gold
Let the loom be placed for me on a square piece of ground.'

128

So Mêng Chiang Nü joined up part with part
Left hand and right hand to and fro unceasing
Upward moving and downward moving, weaving together the *Yin* and
    the *Yang*
On the front of the collar she weaves the lion and seahorse
On the back of the collar the phoenix and unicorn in pairs
On the chest she weaves the Buddhas of old sitting in state
On the back the ancient trees firmly rooted
On the front of the skirt she weaves the brown dragon going down to
    the sea
On the back the Yellow River passing through the Kun Lun mountains
The left-hand sleeve has the blue dragon establishing heaven and earth
The right-hand sleeve the white tiger soaring through the three passes
The seven northern stars and the six southern stars are all woven upon
    the gown
The sun on the left, the moon on the right, surrounded by the bright stars
Now when the purple and gold dragon gown was finished
Mêng Chiang Nü asked the court officials to present it to the Emperor
Chhin Shih Huang Ti saw the gown and was pleased
'This woman is clever, so rare in the whole world'
He sent for the girl to the golden palace
Mêng Chiang Nü went up, sadly pleading
'Your Majesty has listened to my story
Your maidservant is stupid, lacking experience and knowledge
The dragon gown is unsuitable, please pardon it
Now it is finished, please release me to take my husband's body home
So that I can bury it and then wait upon the parents.'
Chhin Shih Huang Ti listened and then spoke thus:
'Mêng Chiang Nü, listen to my words,
The Lonely One loves you who are so good and with your hands so clever
Certainly I will not allow you homeward to go
You must stay with the Lonely One and be made a Lady of Chao Yang.'

You who wish to know how Mêng Chiang Nü took the matter, attend to the
following, and it will be clear:

(*The ballad resumes in seven-character lines as before*)

94. Mêng Chiang Nü : heard the words before the court
    Tears once again : welled up in her two eyes
    Suddenly a plan : entered her heart
    'Your Majesty, be pleased : to grant me an audience

95. If you order me now : to enter your court
    Grant me, thy maidservant : three things only
    For if I lack : but one of the three
    Mêng Chiang Nü prefers to die : here and now.'

96. The wicked Emperor : asked what the three things were
    'Tell me here and now : in person carefully.'
    Mêng Chiang Nü replied : '*First* bury my husband in state
    With jade and gold : as if he were a prince

97. *Second*, let all the state officials mourn : both civil and military
    And Your Majesty, My Lord : carry a hempen stick
    And *Third*, that the burial : be nowhere else
    But upon the shores : of the Eastern Sea

98. These are the three requests : made by thy maiden
    Lacking but one : they will be incomplete.'
    Then the wicked Emperor : listening and smiling
    Promised readily : the three big things

99. 'If you will only : comply with my wishes
    Even seven or eight : would I gladly promise.'
    He then called the court servants : to bring the golden coffin
    Wherein were placed : the bones of the prince

100. He proclaimed that everyone : should put on mourning
     He himself carried : a hempen stick, why not?
     And lastly ordered : the coffin to be borne
     To the shores of the Eastern Sea : there to be buried

101. So everything was ordered : quickly and well
     The bearers of the coffin : marched and marched
     Moving by day : and resting by night
     Until they reached the coast : of the Eastern Sea

102. Then putting down the coffin : they started their labour
     In a place of mountains and waters : true and fitting
     The bier stood ready : the coffin by the tomb
     And Mêng Chiang Nü waiting : by the cliff-temple

103. Finally she knelt : down on the ground
     Prayed to her husband : Fan San-Lang
     'Wait for me : in the other world
     So we may come before : the King of that place together.'

104. When Mêng Chiang Nü had finished : these prayers and orisons
　　Turning round she thanked : the tyrant Emperor
　　For burying her husband : by the Eastern Sea
　　And all the officials : for being present there

105. Having bowed to them all : she knelt down again
　　To her parents for having : nourished and raised her
　　Four prostrations and eight bows : solemnly she gave
　　Did obeisance to the parents-in-law : for their teachings

106. Mêng Chiang Nü was sorry : she could no more wait on them
　　So having thanked all : one by one
　　She turned to the Enlightened One : speaking as follows
　　'Your maidservant Mêng Chiang Nü : is under a vow

107. How can I obey you : O evil King?'
　　Covering up her face : with her skirt of black silk
　　And lifting up her two feet : she leapt into the sea
　　As for the wicked Emperor : he could not stop her.

(*Taoist interpolation; still in seven-character lines*)

　　Now turning from Mêng Chiang Nü : jumping into the sea
　　Let us pass to the court : of the Dragon Sea King
　　The Dragon King soon met : Mêng Chiang Nü
　　Led her to the palace : and enquired what had happened
　　The Dragon Mother seeing her : rejoiced exceedingly
　　Accepted her as daughter : and reported to the Jade Emperor
　　The Jade Emperor thereupon : sent forth his orders
　　This spirit-girl shall be an example : to all generations
　　He gave her wrappings : like the clouds at sunset
　　And set upon her head : the Phoenix crown
　　She was given the spirit-clothes : of the Eight Symbols
　　And a jade girdle : on the wrist, most suitable
　　And shoes for ascending : the clouds in the heavens
　　And the Elixir of Life : and all good heavenly herbs
　　And spirit-tea and spirit-fruit : so that she might never hunger nor thirst
　　Male servants on the left : female on the right
　　Thus in the Heaven-Palace : soon did she sit
　　Surpassing in excellence : all worldly kings
　　The spirit of Fan San-Lang : returned also to the heavens
　　And was made a Golden Boy : for ever and ever
　　Mêng Chiang Nü and San-Lang : keep each other company
　　Thus at last returning : to their first state of being.

(Buddhist interpolation; still in seven-character lines; probably riddles)

One person looking at the compass
Two eyes have no light and cannot suffer the people
Silver teeth inside the mouth bite tight
Determined that the old mother was without birth

Two persons looking at the compass
Caused a *ku-ti* tree to fall down
There is right and wrong; to fight is evil
Those who struggle for fame and money are lost

Three persons looking at the compass
It seemed as if emptiness were ascending upon a white cloud
One wheel of clear wind accompanying the bright moon
Throw away four characters and the God of Fire will burn

Mêng Chiang Nü of course had her own compass
And single-hearted did she follow it
Like the lonely wild geese crying in the empty sky
Invisible was its form
Those who do not fix their hearts like iron
Must act very quickly when danger comes near
Truly like wildfire burning the body
And causing pain without apparent cause
Mêng Chiang Nü suffered and cultivated herself truly
And became an example to all generations
If following this road and learning from enlightened priests
Still the heart is not clear, a man will never see the truth

Mêng Chiang Nü accomplished her work, and lived a virtuous life
After death she went to pay visit to her ancestors
If men and women lived such a good life
They would not die in vain
San-Lang and Mêng Chiang, leaving this earthly existence,
As husband and wife attained their true selfhood
Now, to say no more about the two on their heavenly thrones,
Let us continue with the wicked Emperor Chhin Shih Huang Ti.

(The ballad resumes, as before)

108. The wicked Emperor stood mazed : at Mêng Chiang Nü's act
He had not expected : she would jump into the sea
His eyes gazed in front of him : with never a wink
His mouth opened in anger : and his face turned yellow

109. At last he said : 'This is well fated
    With power you caused the Lonely One : to come to this coast
    It was not that you were unwilling : to bide with him
    But that you wanted : to keep your vows

110. The beauty of your body : was overwhelming
    Your good and faithful heart : was lovely and pitiable
    To live alone for love : is rare in the world
    There are very few girls like this : now to be found

111. Let a monument of stone : be erected on this coast
    In memory of Mêng Chiang Nü : who jumped into the sea
    And now make ready : my chariot royal
    For I will soon return : into my Court.'

10

—————

JOB THE PAYNIM

Address at the Commemoration of Benefactors in Gonville and Caius College
Chapel, 27 October, 1963

In *Acts of the Apostles* we read (10:34)

Then Peter opened his mouth and said: 'Of a truth I perceive that God is
no respecter of persons; but in every nation he that feareth him and worketh
righteousness is accepted with him. . . .'
While Peter yet spake these words, the Holy Ghost fell on all of them which
heard the word. And they of the Circumcision which believed were astonished,
as many as came with Peter, because that on the Gentiles also was poured out
the gift of the Holy Ghost, for they heard them speak with tongues and magnify
God. . . .

Our annual Commemoration of Benefactors now is ended, and
well indeed have we done to offer thanks and praise for the safe
preservation of our ancient and religious foundation through
more than 600 years. Today, in the age of nuclear weapons, our
fears and hopes are perhaps more intense than ever. But in celebrating, quite rightly, our appointed anniversary day, it will do
no harm to remind ourselves that our college, though a whole in
itself, is also a part of a higher-level social organism, and that
again is part of a wider whole – nothing less than the onward
march of cultural achievement, as wide as humanity itself. Local
pride and local patriotism are good in their way, so long as they
do not turn into Pride itself, which despises people of other sorts
who ought to be seen to be our friends and brothers, or into self-
esteem or that self-righteousness of which Professor Lampe spoke

in this place a week ago. Would that we could all say, with Sir Thomas Browne:

I thank God, amongst those millions of Vices I do inherit and hold from Adam, I have escaped one, and that a mortal enemy to Charity, the first and father-sin, not onely of man, but of the devil, Pride; a vice whose name is comprehended in a Monosyllable, but in its nature not circumscribed with a World.

It is good to remember, therefore, that our own pious founders were not the only men, and that Christendom was not the only culture, to set on foot great and noble institutions of learning where successive generations of students assembled to get the benefit of education and research. When the men of Alexander the Great came to Taxila in India in the fourth century B.C. they found a university there the like of which had not then been seen in Greece, a university which taught 'the three Vedas and the eighteen accomplishments' and was still existing when the Chinese pilgrim Fa-Hsien went there about A.D. 400. Later the torch of learning moved to Buddhist Nālanda in Bihar, as we know from the account of that other great pilgrim Hsüan-Chuang in the seventh century. In China the foundation of the Imperial University goes back to 165 B.C. and by the beginning of the Christian era it had no less than 3,000 students. This Kuo Tzu Chien (the College of the Sons of the Nation) remained in being through all the centuries down to our own, and was the fore-runner of the great Chinese universities of today such as Pei Ta and Chhinghua Ta. Some five years ago I myself stood before a splendid inscribed stone monument at Loyang dated A.D. 278 commemorating the re-endowment of the university by the emperor Chin Wu Ti; there were lists of names both of professors and students some of whom came from 'east of the seas' and others from 'west of the shifting sands'.

Nor was specialized education lacking. How fascinated our own John Caius would have been to know that the establishment of an Imperial Medical College was decreed by the emperor of the Northern Wei, Hsiao Wên Ti, in A.D. 493. By 629 it had a branch in every provincial capital, and (believe it or not) we know the sort of questions that were asked in its qualifying examination papers of 758.

Lastly we would naturally expect from Islam, home of that provocative saying 'the ink of science is more precious than the blood of martyrs', something great and enduring in the genre of learned institutions. And indeed we know of the Fātimid foundation, the university of al-Azhar in Egypt, which from A.D. 975 until this day, has taught the arts and sciences of Arabic culture. The place where Ibn Yūnus observed, al-Haitham experimented and Ibn Khaldūn lectured, is now being reformed and vitalized for its task in the contemporary world. Thus the charitable bestowal of goods for the furtherance of education, religion, learning and research, is a pattern common to all civilization, and those 'others whose bounty and wisdom deserve our thankful remembrance' (in the words of our Commemoration service) may perhaps have come from wider regions than we would ever have imagined.

How are we to look upon all these achievements of people who were neither British, nor European, neither Christian, nor 'white'? Surely it can only be with appreciation, indeed with admiration. Truly 'God is no respecter of persons'. Today, at a time when international political tensions are intermingled with racial factors, it is more than ever essential that we approach people of other cultures with the conviction that they have at least as much to give to us as we have to give to them. I remember being deeply impressed by the contrast I found between two great representatives of our country in the early nineteenth-century days of British dominion in India, Lord Macaulay and Sir William Jones. Of his voyage out in 1834 Macaulay wrote to his sister:

> My power of finding amusement without companions was pretty well tried on my voyage. I read insatiably – the Iliad and Odyssey, Virgil, Horace, Caesar's Commentaries, Bacon *De Augmentis*, Dante, Petrarch, Ariosto, Tasso, Don Quixote, Gibbon's Rome ... all the seventy volumes of Voltaire ...

Everything conceivable, in fact, was on board in his crate of books except material which would have given him some elementary ideas of the social systems and religious philosophies of the millions of people he was on his way to govern. After that there is nothing surprising in his famous 'Minute on Indian Education'. Yet just half a century earlier Sir William Jones had set a brilliant example of the opposite kind, of which we can still be proud today. When he went out to be Judge of the High Court in Calcutta in 1783 he had already learnt Arabic and Hebrew at school and Persian and Turkish at Oxford, but after he arrived he became the first Englishman to become a master of Sanskrit. When he died in 1794 the pundits wept for him as for hardly any other Westerner, for he had, it was said, an outstanding 'sympathy with orientals and their manner of thought', and 'felt none of the contempt which his English contemporaries showed to the natives of India'. I have no doubt in my own mind as to which of the two was the better Christian.

At a commemoration such as this, therefore, the Caians whose memory I should particularly like to call to mind, are those who also showed this unprejudiced generous acceptance of all human culture as their own. Khalīl the Physician perhaps you will not recognize, yet it was the Arab name of Charles Doughty (1843–1926) that unique traveller-poet, by training a geologist, whose deeply touching words about his Beduin friendships stand beside the last introduction written by T. E. Lawrence. How modern and contemporary it now seems to find Charles McKenzie (1825–62), long a mathematical tutor here before becoming the first Bishop of Central Africa, fighting bravely, though unsuccessfully, in 1858 for the equal rights of African with white settler congregations. The verdict of the official biographers that 'his desire to place black and white on an equality in matters of church government, and his participation in tribal wars, prove him to have been impulsive and lacking in judgment' may not perhaps stand the test of time. Then there was another Caian, also a mathematical tutor, even more romantically strange in destiny, Thomas Manning (1772–1840). An accomplished mathematician, the friend of Richard Porson and Charles Lamb, Manning, we are told, about 1798 'began to brood upon the mysterious empire of China', finally studying medicine and spending two years in Paris to learn Chinese. He left for Canton in 1806, and five years later made a celebrated journey to Lhasa, where as the first English visitor he won the friendship of the Dalai Lama. Later, in 1817, he was to know Peking also, in the secretariat of Lord Amherst's embassy, and finally his great collection of Chinese books forms the core (I believe) of that now in the care of the Royal Asiatic Society in London.[1] We in Caius had also our own Sir William Jones, a *chela* to his *guru*. Cecil Bendall (1856–1906), Fellow and eventually Honorary Fellow, was one of the greatest collectors of Indian manuscripts of his time, and an outstanding exponent of Mahāyāna Buddhism. His 'profound sympathy with everything Indian' was shared, I know, by the last Caian whom I shall mention, Henry T. Francis (1837–1924). When I was an undergraduate Francis still lived, as he had done for decades, in his rooms at the north end of Tree Court. He was a devoted western Orthodox, that is, an Anglican, and I well remember helping him in and out of his stall at celebrations of the liturgy when he was over eighty – yet he had a profound knowledge of the Pali language and had been a leading member of the English team which translated the *Jātaka* birth-stories, or legends of the reincarnations of Gautama Buddha. One of these stories, the *Vedabha Jātaka*, is the origin of the *Pardoner's Tale* in Chaucer, and many of them are full of the most exquisite and moving compassion, a veritable lesson in civilization which many people in this country and all over the West would do well to take to heart today. These are Caians among others who were benefactors to us by their example, men who could say, again with Sir Thomas Browne: 'All places, all airs, make unto me one Countrey; I am in England everywhere, and under any Meridian.'

So let us conclude that happy as we are in the creation and preservation of this our College, and all the blessings which it has given to our predecessors and ourselves, we should think of it as the part and not the whole. And we must think kindly and warmly also of other men and other foundations, howsoever unlike our own they be. I feel sure that Edmund Gonville would have agreed

[1] Subsequently the collection was transferred to the University Library at Leeds.

with his contemporary John Mandeville, who wrote about 1356 just after the foundation of Gonville Hall, speaking of the Brahmins of India: 'And if all it be so that this manner of folk have not the articles of our belief, nevertheless I trow that for their good faith that they have of kind and good intent, God loves them well and holds them to be henceforth well paid for their good living; as he did of Job, the which was a paynim, and none the less his deeds were acceptable to God, as those of a loyal servant. And if all there be many divers laws and divers sects in the world, nevertheless I trow that God evermore loves well all those that serve him in soothfastness, and serve him meekly and truly, and set not by the vainglory of the world; as this folk does, and as Job did.'

I I

AT THE TOMB OF THE PRINCESS

1964

Near Chhien-hsien, north-west of Sian in Shensi, lies the tomb, recently excavated, of a Thang Princess, Yung Thai Kung-Chu, who was strangled at the age of seventeen in A.D.701, for some reason now unknown, by her grandmother the great empress Wu Tsê-Thien. After the death of the empress, the princess was re-buried magnificently by her father in 706.

The sun shines glorious over the plain and the blue distant hills,
As suns have shone and ripened the grain since old Chêng Kuo
Came to these parts to water Wei Pei and build the power of Chhin.
In silent majesty Liang Shan hoards still the tragic empress
And the little tomb below keeps memory of the little girl
Who fell a victim to intrigues of State and never saw life's fullness.
A martyr to the darkness, the grain still in the ground.
But history ripens too, and now in million upon million
Thai Kung-Chu has sprung up again out of the soil;
In trousers and pigtails she studies vectorial calculus,
Devoutly repaints the old frescoes injured by time,
Takes charge of airfield traffic, and on the bridge,
Rings down full steam ahead for the future of China.

Chêng Kuo was the great hydraulic engineer of the third century B.C. who first planned and organized the irrigation of the land north of the Wei River in Shensi (Wei Pei), then part of the princedom of Chhin. It was this State which, so strengthened, conquered the whole of the rest of China and set up the first unified dynasty, that of Chhin, in B.C. 221. Liang Shan is a natural hill rising up out of the gently sloping plain and containing the tomb, still unopened, of the empress Wu Tsê Thien.

12

THE HOUSE OF WISDOM

Address at the Commemoration of Benefactors in Gonville and Caius College
Chapel, 31 October, 1965

In the sixtieth chapter of Isaiah we find the following poem:

1 Arise, shine, for thy light is come, and the glory of the Lord is risen upon *
thee.
2 For behold the darkness shall cover the earth, and thick darkness the
peoples; but the Lord shall arise upon thee, and his glory shall be seen
upon thee . . .
11 Thy gates shall be open continually; they shall not be shut day nor night,
that men may bring unto thee the wealth of the nations, and their kings
along with them . . .
15 I will make thee an eternal excellency, a joy of many generations.
16 . . . I will also make Peace to be thy officer, and Righteousness thy super-
intendent.
18 Violence shall no more be heard in thy land, neither desolation nor destruction within thy borders. Salvation shall be thy city-wall, and Praise
shall be thy gate.

These words, which form part of what is sometimes called the
'Song of Zion redeemed', have had, like all the great prophecies,
many applications. Isaiah meant them no doubt as a description
of what Israel and Jerusalem could be to the world if his people
would really follow God's commandments of social righteousness; then in later generations they were applied as a 'type' of
poetic prefiguration either of the glory of the Christian universal
Church or, more tellingly perhaps, of that Kingdom of God on
earth which the age-long struggles of men for liberty, equality
and fraternity would bring into being. Of course we won't want

to disavow any of these 'types and shadows', but can't we also apply the prophet's wonderful words to social organisms such as our own College, the founders and benefactors of which have been receiving our meed of prayer and remembrance before God this evening? I think we can, and if so, then certain meditations may come into our minds and find a voice.

First, then, these words were not written by a Christian. Isaiah never knew anything about harvest festivals or the U.S.P.G. Perhaps you normally think of people like Isaiah as 'honorary Christians'; but if you are going as far as that, you might well go further and extend the idea to all men of goodwill, the saints and sages of all people that on earth do dwell. The present opportunity is a good one to enlarge our minds, and realize that in the 'Republic of Letters' the setting up of institutions by pious and devoted founders for the advancement of 'education, religion, learning and research' was not an enterprise confined to Christendom, or to Europe, or to so-called 'white' people. All the great civilizations have done this, and in all of them the social organisms so founded have lasted through many centuries, as has our own. Only the dedications differ; the aim has been the same. And often they were ahead of us. Our own Hall of the Annunciation of Blessed Mary the Virgin, commonly called Gonville and Caius College, dates, as we know so well, from 1348; but the College of All Sages, the Chi Hsien Yuan, at the Thang capital of Chhang-an in China, was set up in about 725; and the House of Wisdom, the Beit al-Hikmah, started in Baghdad in 830.

I should like to tell you a little more about the enlightened home of Arabic learning. Its founder was the celebrated caliph al-Mamun in that thrilling period when the Arabs were discovering Greek science and making it their own, before transmitting it in furthered form centuries later to the Latins and Franks, our Western ancestors. The House of Wisdom had lecture rooms and dining halls, a splendid library, two astronomical observatories and, above all, a richly-supported translation bureau. Under the first Master of the House, Ibn Abu-Mansur, the pattern was set for a couple of centuries, with the measurement of the length of the

terrestrial degree, the extraordinary achievements of the Banu
Musa brothers in the mechanical sciences, and above all the
activities of Muhammad al-Khwarizmi, the greatest mathematician of his age in the world and the father of algebra. Meanwhile the translators sat under the physician Hunayn Ibn Ishaq,
the 'sheik of all interpreters', a Nestorian Christian and a most
noble character who once spent a year in prison for refusing to
use his pharmacological knowledge to poison one of the Caliph's
enemies, when commanded to do so. What has this to do with us?
someone may ask. Only that when Edmund Gonville's contemporaries and successors studied Aristotle or Galen, they did it
through texts which had passed into Arabic in the ninth century
and then on into Latin in Muslim Spain in the eleventh and
twelfth. Not till the decline and fall of Byzantium, nearer John
Caius' time, did Western Europeans get access to the original
texts; and then, as we know, Caius himself was expert in them.
Thus it is not at all far-fetched to think of al-Khwarizmi and
Hunayn Ibn Ishaq as among our forefathers that begat us, just as
much as Thomas Bradwardine or Adelard of Bath.

Even more like our College was the Nizamiyah at Baghdad,
which arose in 1065, after the decay of the House of Wisdom, and
just when rough William was taking possession of our land. It
was founded by Nizam al-Mulk, the Persian vizir of the Seljuq
sultans Alp Arslan and Malik Shah, and the patron of a poet well
known to all of us, Umar al-Khayyami. The institution was a real
madrassah, a college, with a great library and hundreds of living-
rooms, with scholarships, with professors, senior lecturers and
junior instructors, so like indeed to the oldest European universities
that many believe it was their very paradigm. The greatest of all
Islamic mystical theologians, al-Ghazzali, taught there towards
the end of the eleventh century, and during Edmund Gonville's
lifetime, in 1327, a graphic description of it was given by the
great traveller Ibn Battutah. The Nizamiyah survived the
Mongolian conquest of 1258 and at the end of the fourteenth
century merged with a younger sister-college the Mustansiriyah.
Unlike Gonville Hall, it was not at all a 'poor house'; it had

admirable baths, a splendid dining hall and kitchens, and a teaching hospital or *bimaristan*. The buildings fortunately still survive, though till lately they were used as a customs warehouse; I hope that the Iraqis are treating them now as a national monument.

Mention of the hospital at Baghdad reminds me of another way in which we have communion with those of other civilizations who were inspired by God to philanthropic actions. The Imperial Medical College in China, the Thai I Hsüeh, first appears as early as 493, when the emperor appointed a Regius Professor of Medicine (Thai I Po-Shih) and a Regius Lecturer (Thai I Chu-Chiao). As soon as the Thang dynasty came in, in 618, this College was enlarged, and by 629 replicated in every provincial capital. By 702 the Japanese emperor followed suit. About the time of the birth of Edmund Gonville, Marco Polo was in China or on his way home, and from the account given in a book called the *Mêng Liang Lu* we know much of the Imperial Medical College at Hangchow, that 'pearl of cities all', a college which Polo may well have visited. It had lecture-halls for each of the four chief professors, a temple for the veneration of the tutelary deities of medicine, and a refectory with excellent food for the 250 students, who were accommodated in eight study-houses, the very names of which have come down to us. They were all equipped with a special coloured cap and belt which distinguished them from ordinary citizens, but they had to face examinations not only every quarter but every month.

Here was something special, a new contribution to civilized life, the protection of the people from the dangerous activities of unqualified practitioners. This was one of the things most dear to the heart of John Caius, whose firm stand in this matter brought him great difficulties and unpopularity during his Presidencies of the Royal College of Physicians. He never knew that in far distant Cathay the first steps had been taken toward this end, before the end of the fifth century. But so it was, and most probably Baghdad was the way-station in the transmission of the idea to Europe. For in 931 the caliph al-Muqtadir decided to license practitioners by examination, entrusting the superintendence of the same to the great physician Sinan Ibn Thabit Ibn Qurrah. Thence, with little doubt, the idea passed westwards to Sicily and Salerno, where in 1140 King Roger decreed qualifying medical examinations for the first time in Europe.

Let us then praise famous men, and our fathers that begat us, not only in our own culture of the Western part of the Old World, but in all the great cultures of the past, for East and West are one. We must remember too that culture has always been in peril, and that men have had to fight to preserve and enlarge it. In the words of Isaiah with which I began there is a grim undertone that we cannot forget. Darkness shall cover the earth, and thick darkness the peoples. There is mention of violence, desolation and destruction. What would he have said if he could have known of the potentialities of nuclear weapons; the special darkness of our time? Here in this chapel, where we have met in seeming peace and tranquillity to celebrate this anniversary, we are perhaps too little mindful of the sufferings that our fellow men and fellow scholars are undergoing in many parts of the world, I think especially of the tragedy of Vietnam. There the whole culture of a relatively unarmed Asian people is in danger; fearful force is being applied to them to make them follow a Western path, by men who in their ruthless pride consider the way of life of the West to be the only rightful way of life. I agree with the Bishop of Llandaff who said, in an excellent letter to *The Times* last March, that the burning alive of men, women and children with napalm was not exactly the way to commend Christian civilization (or capitalism for that matter) to an Asian people, whose own age-old traditions had embodied neither. We are too much tempted to a 'fearful acquiescence' in the deeds which are done in our name. Among religious people in Cambridge, and in College chapels too, there is still, I suspect, too much emphasis on individual personal salvation, and too little sense of responsibility for what Christendom does as a whole. But we must hope that this agony in South-east Asia will soon be over, and do all we can ourselves to end it. Tonight, at least, we are thinking in a social context, and our company, our society, those of us who happen to be here now, those that have gone before, and those who will follow us within this social organism, are united before the heavenly throne.

The older I grow, the more I find something consoling in the perennial quality of a home of learning and teaching such as our College has been and is. No individual is irreplaceable or indispensable; we all contribute as best we can, but it is something so much more than us, and it will go on without us. If any one of us should by God's will at any time be taken away, the bell will ring for hall and chapel just the same; the others will continue to study, think and worship. And even though the social organisms are themselves far from eternal, new forms will arise as others die, within the unity of all mankind. And so very reasonably we may turn and say:

O God, who at sundry times and in divers places hast impelled faithful men to establish homes and halls for the advancement of truth and its transmission from generation to generation, look favourably, we pray Thee, upon this our community, and prosper it in all its works, through Jesus Christ our Lord, who with the Father and the Holy Spirit showeth forth the perfect mystery of the common life unto ages of ages. Amen.

13

SCIENCE AND
PEACE—THE ASIAN ASPECT

First published in *Science for Peace Bulletin*, October 1951

This theme, as it stands, is vague. There are doubtless many ways in which it can be made concrete. Here I suggest that it should be thought of in the context of what is perhaps the greatest social movement of our times, the resurgence of Asia. The benefits which post-Renaissance science and technology have brought to human life are now fully appreciated by the greater and 'under-privileged' part of the world's population, and there is a determination, entirely understandable, to participate in them. A great responsibility rests on scientific workers in the most advanced countries to recognize these aspirations of the Asian peoples, to help them in their struggle, to seek to understand their difficulties with sympathy, and to explain to our occidental fellow-citizens the vital part which the liberation of Asia from servitude to famine, disease and exploitation, is playing in the preservation of world peace.

In July of last year *The Times* published a letter from me deploring the destruction by bombing of the industrial plants of North Korea. Avoiding legal arguments about the origin of the Korean war, I tried to point out that the occidental common-wealths had adopted policies which were bound to make them seem, to the Asian peoples, the enemies of that technological advancement which alone can raise the standard of life in that continent to minimal decent levels. Since that time the position has steadily worsened. Each step on the downward path towards another world war is accepted with a regret which soon gives place to indifference or resignation until the next crisis arises. Despite the prevailing attitude of both government and opposition spokesmen, as well as most of the press, I believe that a substantial minority of the people of this country are not in agreement with it.

Sir Robert Craigie, in *The Times* for May 9th last, argued the case for economic sanctions against China in a way which no doubt satisfied the majority of his readers, who themselves would have had no first-hand acquaintance with the dire poverty of the masses of Asian people, and would be unwilling even to try to imagine it. They were told that sanctions, trade embargoes, and even naval blockade, would not increase the danger of war because China's war potential is negligible. Danger to Hongkong was discounted on the ground that it is indefensible anyway, and 'appeasement' was considered unnecessary since China would never wish to become fully a satellite of the Soviet Union. But it is high time that someone said what many people think, that the entire 'tough-minded' attitude towards Asia, together with the false historical analogy of 'appeasement', cloaks a fundamentally immoral policy for which this country may have to pay dearly in years to come.

According to the Report of a U.S. Senate Commission in 1947, a population of 150 million in Western Europe enjoys a per capita annual income of $400 U.S. The 200 million people in Eastern Europe have a standard of life equivalent to an annual income of $120 U.S. The 1,300 million people of Asia have an average standard equivalent to only $30 U.S. Again, Asia, with 57 per cent of the world's population, has only 11 per cent of the total world power production. Such figures can be paralleled by others for availability of goods and services of every description. If embargoes and blockades are applied to Asian countries, does anyone really suppose that the 'astute Chinaman' (as Sir Robert calls him) will believe that this is well-merited punishment for disobedience to a United Nations in which one of the two greatest Asian powers has long been deliberately denied representation? Will he not rather take it as crowning evidence of occidental hostility, not to his government only, but to his deepest aspirations and demands for a reasonable standard of life and all that that implies? It is of course being said that the embargo applies only to war materials, but in fact in most cases it is impossible to distinguish between materials of strategic and non-strategic value. Restriction of trade in rubber may indeed mean that one Chinese soldier the less will have a rainproof coat with which to confront the Korean weather (and the American jellied petrol), but it will also mean that the Chinese miner and ferryman will have to continue to work barefoot. Last year the most highly industrialized nations in the world engaged in the systematic destruction of the nascent industries of one of the least highly industrialized. Now the wealthiest nations are planning, to the accompaniment of sustained applause in the columns of our most responsible newspapers, the more thorough deprivation of the already deprived.

The inevitable answer which makes itself heard is that however much we may dislike it, we are tied hand and foot to the policies of the United States, which alone can protect West Europe from attack by the Soviet Union. Let us concede, for argument's sake, that there is a risk of this. Is not the rise of the entire continent of Asia in a 'holy war' against the West a risk far greater? Of course, as is sometimes said, it does not matter

> . . . for we have got
> The atom bomb, and they have not . . .

Yet if all the high-sounding talk about 'collective security' is leading the rich quarter of the world's population to a position in which it must literally destroy the under-privileged and technically undeveloped three-quarters – then what began as a doctrine to preserve peace will end as a war to preserve the technical superiority and wealth of the white race. If such a concept as the sin of nations is still legitimate, is this not something very like it? And will it not ultimately bring its inevitable wages?

We constantly hear it said by scientists of unquestionable eminence that the pursuit of truth and natural knowledge is a full-time job, leaving no time for social or political considerations. It would be presumptuous, they affirm, to suppose that scientific qualifications give the scientist any ground upon which to speak to his fellow-citizens. For the young, the scales are weighted as heavily as ever, if not indeed more heavily than before, in favour of assent, conformity and convention. But we persist in our conviction that the scientific view of the world does give the scientist a particular public duty which no other citizens can so well fulfil. Let him, then, study, among other aspects of our present world, the problems posed by the resurgence of the Asian peoples, and if he should find that the way to world peace involves the extension to all mankind of the benefits of modern science and technology, let him assert this and endeavour to explain to his fellow-citizens the consequences of it.

14

THE FRAGRANCE OF FRIENDSHIP

Address at the inaugural meeting of the
Society for Anglo-Chinese Understanding
15 May, 1965

It is a great honour, as well as a pleasure, for me to be asked to open
this meeting today, designed to set on foot an organization for
fostering friendship and mutual understanding between the British
and the Chinese peoples, on a far broader basis than hitherto. The
stature and magnitude of Chinese culture, the way of life of nearly
a quarter of the whole human race, is today, as *The Times* has
recently said, a dominant fact of international relationships which
has to be reckoned with. China is no longer something quaint,
something archaic, unimportant and irrelevant. The event reported
in this morning's papers [the second Chinese nuclear test] is
witness of this. Largely by their own efforts the Chinese are
raising their standard of life to a proper level. They have thrown
off the inhibitions of their traditional social forms, and are taking
a place on the modern world stage which will be second to none.
An immense reservoir of talent has been released; it will make an
enormous contribution to world civilization. China can no longer
be for us some 'little country far away about which we know
nothing', for in these days of air communications China is only
about a dozen hours' flying time away. Neighbours need to be
good friends. The smaller our world becomes, the greater is the
urgency of mutual understanding of the peoples and their cultures.
    The keynote of what I have to say today may perhaps be found
in that phrase which was used by Andrea Corsalis when he wrote
from China in A.D. 1515 to Lorenzo de Medici saying that the
Chinese were 'of great skill' and *di nostra qualità* – of the same

calibre as ourselves. It is interesting to note that this had been
appreciated by the Chinese too more than a thousand years
earlier, when the author of the *Wei Lüeh* wrote in the third
century A.D. that 'the people of Ta-Chhin (that is the Roman
Empire), are tall, upright in their dealings like us Chinese, but
wear a different dress'. Again, when Vasco da Gama had rounded
the Cape of Good Hope and arrived with his crews on the east
coast of Africa, they heard that fair-skinned mariners had been
there long before, and indeed it was true that the Portuguese of
1496 had been anticipated by Chinese fleets and merchants during
the previous couple of centuries. The great poet Camoens in his
epic *Os Lusiados* wrote concerning the Arab pilots who gave
this news:

> In the Arabick-Tongue (which they speak ill,
> But Fernand Martyn understandeth though)
> They say, in Ships as great as those we fill,
> That sea of theirs is travers't to and fro,
> Even from the rising of the Sun, untill
> The Land makes Southward a Full Point, and so
>   Back from the South to East; conveying, thus,
>   Folks of the colour of the Day, like Us.

In my own personal experience I have lived through the same
discovery that these others made so long before. During the
thirties I was fortunate enough to win the friendship of some of
the Chinese scientists who came to Cambridge to work for their
research degrees, and so it was that I took up the study of the
language and the culture, in the first place quite as a hobby. My
own experience with them, and with the hundreds or even
thousands of Chinese whom I subsequently met, convinced me
that the more I got to know them the more exactly like myself
they seemed to be, allowing always of course for the refreshing
differences of cultural tradition. And so it came about that when in
1942 I found myself at Kunming in south-west China entrusted
with a mission of scientific and technological liaison between the
Chinese and the Western Allies, I immediately felt completely
at home in the laboratories of my Chinese colleagues, men

like Thang Phei-Sung and Ching Li-Pin and Wu Yu-Hsün, evacuated as they then were to the country round about this second wartime capital. In a word, the more you get to know the Chinese the more you will like them.

One must always remember however that China is not simply a different country from our own, like Rumania, for instance, or the Argentine, but a basically different civilization. There is thus a much greater gulf of fundamental assumptions to be bridged, as well as all the fascinating differences that arise in philosophy, art, landscape, language, religion, customs, and so on. This requires a real effort towards understanding, the very purpose of our new Society. The intense feeling of unity which I have mentioned arises perhaps especially naturally in the relations between scientists or mathematicians or engineers but I believe that everyone in their way can share this, whether architects or dockers, farmers or physicians, and for this reason alone I am convinced that far more personal contacts are necessary and urgent between these civilizations.

There are many ideas in the Western mind about Chinese people and their culture, but there is no time to discuss them much today. I should like to refer, however, to what in my own mind I think of as the Whopping Lie Department. 'All Chinese are inscrutable', 'Chinese people look exactly alike', 'Chinese names all sound the same, and no one can remember them', 'you can never tell what they are thinking or what they intend' – all this belongs to the category which Claude Roy has so well called 'the iron curtain of false enigmas'. It is variously said that the Chinese have consisted only of peasants and craftsmen, that they never had any science, they knew nothing of formal logic, they had no historiography, they possess no sense of time, they have never been curious about the works of Nature or the cultures of other countries. I suppose that all this nonsense can only be overcome by effort ever renewed, by personal contact, by the generation of sympathy, in a word by friendly acts of mutual recognition, of equality, of dignity, as in the quotations with which I began.

Worse than the Whopping Lie Department is the Plausible

Half-Truth Department, because its pronouncements don't always sound so ridiculous. Half-truths often arise from a failure of historical perspective and this has got to be corrected too. As an example, one might take a recent television programme which purported to be a humanistic and sympathetic account of the Chinese in Hongkong; perhaps it was intended as a joke, but it could very easily be misunderstood as a piece of racialism when the programme was said to be 'confined to people who *know* that they are the superior race on earth, because they were born Chinese'. Now there is a sense in which the Chinese have had a superiority complex, if I may call it such, instead of an inferiority complex; actually they had both at once. The prestige of Chinese humanistic culture was so great that it overshadowed all the other cultures of the East Asian geographical area. During the war, though material conditions in China were still largely medieval (very different to those of the present day), this prestige was still omnipresent in the atmosphere, and I used to say at the Embassy in the war years that a post in China was the ideal thing for a young member of the Foreign Service. In Chungking, a young Third Secretary, instead of being regarded on all hands as the salt of the earth, would have to spend a lot of his time in explaining that he was not some kind of outer barbarian, and I thought this would be very good for him. Ancient and medieval China, of course, adopted the expression Chung-Kuo, 'the central country', for their nation-state, and this term is still used in common speech. But at the present day the Chinese are, in my opinion, among the most internationally-minded people anywhere on earth. Even in the remotest parts of the country the people know the sufferings of the days of imperialism and colonialism, and everywhere they have a deep and real sympathy with the people throughout the world who are trying to liberate themselves today from those conditions.

Another example might be taken from the growth of humanitarianism. The expression 'Chinese torture' has become proverbial, but in fact it dates only from the early decades of the nineteenth century, the time of the Opium Wars, when expanding capitalism and commerce were battering at the seaward gates of China. If you go back to the early sixteenth century, when the first Portuguese traders arrived, you get an entirely different picture. Instead of exclaiming at the barbarousness of punishments (which were like those of Europe) and the inadequacies of the magistrates, the Portuguese were never tired of singing the praises of the laws and government of China; and they knew what they were talking about because quite a number of them saw the inside of Chinese prisons. Coastal trading was then under government supervision and they freely broke the rules of it. Now, of course, the Chinese are just as humanitarian as anyone else. Thus something had happened in those 300 years to hold back China to the Middle Ages while Europe went ahead into the modern world. One may ask what this was? It was, I believe, the fact that modern science grew up in Europe, and in Europe alone, *modern* science with all the technology and ideology which flowed from it. I am sure that the growth of humanitarianism was connected with this growth of science.

People who say that the Chinese had no science are again talking nonsense because they have no historical perspective. Between the first and fifteenth centuries A.D., Chinese science and technology was often far ahead of Europe. They had a lead of thirteen centuries, for example, in the art of making cast iron, and some six centuries in the invention of the mechanical clock. Wisdom was therefore not born with us, as Europeans so commonly assume. The point is that China went on her slow upward way without the vast upheavals of the Renaissance, the Reformation, and the rise of capitalism, out of which modern science came into being in the West. If people would only read a little more history they would not talk (as they sometimes do) about the Asian peoples as stealing away the results of modern science from those who were its real creators. *Modern* science began in Europe in the time of Galileo, it is true, but all the nations and the peoples have contributed to science *as such*, the foundations on which the men of the scientific revolution built, and here no people were more outstanding than the Chinese.

By a parallel train of thought it is often said that China is now 'Westernizing' herself. This conception is freely used even by some learned men, but I think they are deeply mistaken. To the term 'modernization' I should not object, but I believe that the age-old traditions of Confucianism and Taoism are still now, and always will remain, the background of Chinese mentality – as Christianity is of our mentality in the West. Particular play is made with the idea that China has taken as her chief inspiration from the West the philosophy of Marxism, something which germinated, it is maintained, only a stone's throw from here in the British Museum Library. People who say this simply could not be more wrong. The perennial philosophy of Chinese culture was from the beginning an organic materialism which left very little place for idealistic systems. In my view the leading philosophical thinkers of China throughout the ages would have welcomed dialectical materialism most warmly if they had known of it, and would have regarded it as an extension of the characteristic Chinese mode of thought. Indeed, there is some historical evidence for the view that the ideas of Chinese organic materialism entered European thinking by the intermediation of the Jesuit Mission in the seventeenth century, bearing fruit in the West from Leibniz onwards. So it was not in the least surprising that the Chinese intelligentsia adopted dialectical materialism with such unanimity.

Besides what we have already said, there is also of course the Department of Bland Ignorance. Yet there are certain things which it is really urgent to understand about China and to make better understood. As I have already indicated, there was no indigenous development of capitalism in that civilization. There was therefore no obvious reason in the present century why China should go through all the stages of capitalist development. Capitalism was something essentially foreign which the Chinese themselves had never generated, did not understand, and came to want less and less. In the twenties therefore it was natural that there should be much discussion about whether China would not be better advised to go straight to a socialist organization of society. Indeed one could almost subsume the whole of Chinese history in this century by saying that it was the gradual but irrevocable decision of this vast people to omit the capitalist stage of economic development and pass straight to socialism and ultimately communism.

Here again it is extremely important that Westerners should understand how different Chinese feudalism was from Western European feudalism. Instead of the hereditary aristocratic principle which we had, the Chinese had a different form, which may be described as bureaucratic. China was governed by a non-hereditary élite, the mandarinate in fact, whose world view differed deeply from those of the aristocrat and of the merchant. The *carrière ouverte aux talents* was a Chinese invention, not a French one. There is a certain philosophical likeness between the government of China today and the government that China has always had, while of course the fundamental aims of imperial government and of contemporary socialist government are utterly and irreconcilably different.

If there was relatively little idealistic metaphysics in China, at the same time there was little transcendental religion. The Tao of the Taoists was immanent, the Way of the sage Confucius was incarnate in human society – even in Buddhism there was no divine creator or law-giver. Was it not perhaps for these reasons that China shows throughout her history almost no persecution for religious opinions? Surely this is a very significant fact to compare with our own abundance of martyrdoms, and the activities of the Holy Inquisition. I believe this sort of thing has much to do with the immense emphasis placed on persuasion in the China of our own times. In the 'leading with an open hand', as John Gray has well said, we are seeing 'the ideals of the first Communist leadership to have had a Confucian education'.

Of course one could go on indefinitely on these lines. One might refer to what I call the Random Phrase Department, the picking out of isolated aphorisms and the drawing of conclusions from them. If a famous Chinese writer makes the 'off the cuff' remark that the Chinese always either enslaved or fought foreigners and never attempted diplomacy, he must not be quoted in isolation, for the notion is historically indefensible. Embassies were coming and going throughout Chinese history from the time of the Huns in the second century B.C. to that of the Jesuits and Russians in the seventeenth century A.D. Indeed we owe to the diaries of these envoys many a precious piece of information about the neighbouring countries in Asia during the Middle Ages. Similarly another Chinese writer is quoted as having said on one occasion that the Chinese always treated foreigners either as animals or overlords and never as friends; but this was a Shavian provocation which all history denies. Indeed there were times, for instance during the Thang period, when exotic foreigners of every kind, the Nestorian priest and the Persian alchemist, were the height of fashion in Chinese society. Long before that time the invading northern nomadic houses who set up dynasties in various parts of China became completely absorbed in Chinese society as time went by, and many intimate friendships and mixed unions were part of the process. Later on, in the Yuan period, foreigners were again in demand as experts of all kinds, both in and out of the administration (like Marco Polo himself), and the process was repeated in the case of the learned astronomical Jesuits (the only foreigners who ever achieved the distinction of having their biographies inserted in the dynastic history). This was an example of cultural intercourse at the highest level, and later it was echoed by the work of the Anglo-Saxon missionaries of the nineteenth century.

I do not think it is necessary for me now to summarize the aims and objectives of the Society for Anglo-Chinese Understanding. These are set forth in various statements which you have. The point in a nutshell is that the British people and the Chinese people must come to know each other better. It is urgently necessary for our understanding of world affairs today that the Chinese point of view on all kinds of matters, political as well as cultural, should be made known. We want to do this without preconceived bias or ideological inhibitions, yet not necessarily without constructive comment and sympathetic criticism. The Society will be, as I see it, non-political, in that it is not designed for direct political action, but it will be concerned with politics in the sense that we want to know and make known what the Chinese think and say about them, especially having in mind the basically humanistic and altruistic aims of the society which they are building in their country. All our activities will be directed towards the objective of getting to know China and our Chinese friends better. All we need to start from is a friendly frame of mind. If this object can be achieved we shall be making a great contribution to the development of world peace and international comprehension.

May I in conclusion remind you of three phrases which we might inscribe upon the banners of the organization now arising, watchwords indicating the attitude we ought to have towards our task. All come from the Chinese classics. The first one is: 'He who comes with the odour of enmity will invite the clash of weapons, he who comes with the fragrance of friendship will be loved like a brother.' Next I will quote the words *san jen hsing pi yu wo shih*: 'Where three men are walking together it is certain that one or other of them will be able to teach me something.' And lastly that great doctrine *ssu hai chih nei, chieh hsiung ti yeh*: 'Within the four seas all men are brothers.'

I5

A POEM FOR A CHINESE FRIEND

1946, first printed in *Science Outpost*, 1948

Conductor's rod erect
Violins and horns await the flash
The thunder of the opening bars
Lighting the landscape of the symphony.
But there are two (at least) of these
Two landscapes, two symphonies, two composers,
Chung and Hsi
China and Europe.

It is true the basic melodies are the same
Mêng Chiang Nü and the Wars in High Germany
The Girl Selling Chiaodze and the Collier's Daughter
(Ascetics and materialists
Sceptics and Pelagians, all are there)
But the scores are written so differently
Ku-chin and pi-pa against 'cello and flute
That hardly anyone listens to both
And few there are who cross the barrier to and fro.

Barriers of deserts and jungles
Barriers of snow-mountains and empty ocean
For three thousand years hiding
The houses of Han and Thang,
Few there were, and few there are, coming and going.
And there is only one competent camel-guide, truck-driver, airpilot
Love;
Otherwise, No road going,
No planes flying.

A Poem for a Chinese Friend

And have we not seen it so –
Indignation against oppression and misery, raising
A technical school for flesh and blood in a sandy city –
Investigation year after weary year by the student of plague
Dissecting endemic rats and fleas in a bamboo shed –
Iron and steel to the help of the million families
('You may call me if you like a metallurgical missionary') –
Inspiration of universal faith
Keeping a Cantonese bishop always on the road –
Intellectual passion of the sinologist
Lovingly tracing the characters on the oracle-bones.

As for us, at our back there are flags
(Like the generals in the play
Smoothing their beards
Brandishing their knees and shaking out their fans)
Zürich and Eltisley, Bala and Coutances
Ringstead Mill and Mantes-la-Jolie,
Mount Konocti and Santa Barbara,
Huangshansse and Taipinglu,
These are our battle-honours.
You stood in Marchwood churchyard
I burnt incense to your ancestors.

And so the endless conversation went on –
'In the Yuan dynasty
Hu Sse-Hui clearly distinguished between the two forms of beriberi'
'The life of the merchant city-state
Included no magistrate appointed by an emperor'
'The opinion of Aristotle was . . .'
'As Su Tung-Po says . . .'
The eternal approximation to unity,
Two miraculously become one.

And for me, in the face of things difficult to understand
You, the Explainer, the Antithesis, *
(whether or not in the flesh)
Were always there,

You, the outward and tangible sign
Of the strength of all workers' muscles under the hot sun
Intelligence of scholars attending to brush-strokes
Beauty of all Chinese women under the moon.
You, the manifestation of what Lucretius invokes:
QUAE QUONIAM RERUM NATURA SOLA GUBERNAS
The assurance of a link
No separation can break.

As it is written in the Book of Rites
THIEN HSIA TA THUNG
All under Heaven shall be One Community.

16

WESTERN MISCONCEPTIONS
ABOUT EAST ASIA

An address at Norwich, 1967

The war in Vietnam is stirring the conscience of our country as it has not been stirred for a long time past, and many consider that the Labour Government's support for the American actions in Vietnam is the most shameful example of Britain's 'satellite' status that has yet been given. Others, convinced that what they regard as the only possible conception of 'freedom' necessarily depends upon capitalist economics, applaud the proceedings of the Americans, and look on them as a necessary holding action in the semi-Cold War. But hardly anyone on either side takes the trouble to study certain fundamental characteristics of East Asian sociological history. This, of course, does not prevent them from drawing conclusions based on assumptions about these. I should like to take this opportunity of examining some of these assumptions.

As is well known, the culture of the Vietnamese people is essentially Chinese. They belong to the north-eastern side of that line which runs through the Indo-Chinese sub-continent dividing the cultures primarily Indian from those primarily Chinese. But 'Chinese culture', we hear it said, 'has always been basically expansionist and imperialist; if Vietnam were to go communist, there would be no hope for Malaya and India'. This attitude simply ignores 2,000 years of Chinese history. The remarkable thing about it, when closely studied, is how China refrained through the ages • from imposing rule on the neighbouring peoples of the culture-area.

China proper forms a great natural *Lebensraum* into which the Chinese people from Shang times onward (second millennium B.C.) expanded outwards from the Yellow River Valley, absorbing as they went the related tribal peoples of mountains and forests. This process stopped to the west at the foot of the Tibetan mountains, to the north at the edge of the Gobi desert and the Manchurian steppe, to the south at the forests and jungles of Vietnam, to the east at the ocean. Korea and Vietnam share a certain pattern in their history – both were partly incorporated as regular prefectures by China in the Han period (second century B.C. to second century A.D.), but left to their own devices thereafter. Nearly two thousand years of Korean and Vietnamese independence saw only occasional armed quarrel with China, and no concerted effort to absorb them. Again, Japan, a culture which exactly resembled those of Korea and Vietnam in looking to China as the home of light and learning, and in utilizing the Chinese written script for its own quite different language, was never attacked with a view to forcible incorporation in the Chinese empire. Only the Mongolians attempted this, towards the end of the thirteenth century A.D., with results closely paralleling the fate of the Spanish Armada.

The case of Tibet, which has been made unnecessarily controversial, is rather different; its relation with China proper resembles that of Wales or Aquitaine to England, involving medieval feudal history. The Mongolians assumed the Protectorate of Lamaist Buddhism, consequently when their rulers the Great Khans became the emperors of China in the Yuan dynasty, the overlordship of the Tibetan theocracy reverted to the Chinese state. This the Tibetans have never denied, and other nations, including Britain, have always accepted it.

Broadly speaking, the Chinese system was always one of tribute states – never colonizing anywhere or planting forts and people. On occasion the Chinese were capable of extraordinary military expeditions, notably one across Tibet in the eighteenth century to induce Nepal to continue paying tribute, which it successfully did, but these were exceptional.

An outstanding contrast is provided between the Chinese explorations in the Indian Ocean in the first half of the fifteenth century A.D., and the actions of the Portuguese there somewhat later. It is not generally known, perhaps, that just as the Portuguese were exploring down the west coast of Africa, the Chinese were trading and treating with the whole of the east coast, the Arabic emirates of al-Zanj – as well as with Arabia itself and all of India, Malaya and Indonesia. The Portuguese carried war at its most cruel into these regions, with a mentality still fixed in that of the Crusades, and their persecution of the 'heathen' makes depressing reading today. But the Chinese everywhere set up no forts, founded no colonies, attempted no conversions, established no inquisitions; they sought nothing but acknowledgment of tribute status and intensive trading under the guise of exchange of state gifts. There can be no question which were the more civilized, the Far Westerners or the Far Easterners.

Then in the nineteenth century the diaspora. The man in the street today, seeing large Chinese populations in Singapore, Malaya, the West Indies, the Guianas, San Francisco and elsewhere, thinks naturally of some kind of 'colonization'. He should understand that these people were not sent out by China, they were rather 'sucked out' by the vacuum demand for cheap labour occurring at a certain stage in the development of capitalist industry and cash crop agriculture – the building of the American trans-continental railways, the phosphate mining on Christmas Island, or the open-cast tin in Malaya. This was the result of modern science and industry, very much ahead in these places as compared to China herself.

Chinese culture has not, therefore, been basically expansionist and imperialist; the facts are exactly the opposite. China was, of course, an 'empire' for some three thousand years, but paradoxically a 'non-imperialist' one – if we use the word imperialism in its modern capitalist context.

One word here about the population problem. China at the present day is not as over-populated as India by any means. Since 1952 I have been in People's China three times, and have on each occasion looked into the attitudes on this question. Fifteen years ago it was felt that the vast empty spaces in Manchuria, Mongolia, Kansu and Sinkiang, would suffice for the population increase for half a century to come without control, but now this opinion is being revised. Contraceptive measures have been sometimes positively urged in government health propaganda, sometimes not, but always I have found contraceptives freely on sale in the department stores and co-operative shops. Population control will assuredly come in China.

Chinese culture and Chinese state power, then, will certainly not spread outwards beyond their traditional boundaries. But the ideas of socialism and communism are quite another matter. They may have a profound attraction for the under-developed countries of Asia (and elsewhere). Is it the duty of the West to stop this by fire and sword? This brings me to the second fundamental misconception which I perceive in the minds of Westerners who are ignorant of Asian history. 'Of course,' they say, 'Chinese and East Asian society should normally be "free" and capitalist; whatever hampers this is diabolically engineered from somewhere' (hardly nowadays Moscow). 'And so it is our right and duty to see that development in Asia keeps to the normal paths of social evolution, not "deviating" into socialism and communism.'

This is a complete misunderstanding. China, the greatest of the East Asian nations and their permanent paradigm, did not spontaneously develop capitalist institutions. They were thrust upon her, in very imperfect form, during the relatively short period of Western dominance and 'semi-colonialism' during the late nineteenth and early twentieth centuries. Between medieval China and medieval Europe there were profound sociological differences, the greatest being that while the latter had that military aristocratic feudalism with which we are all familiar, the former had a civilian bureaucratic feudalism, that of the mandarinate and the civil service examinations. The European social system seemed strong, but in reality it was very weak, permitting the rise of mercantile and then industrial capitalism within itself as the times ripened; the former seemed weak, but in reality it was extremely strong (perhaps because more rational fundamentally), and capable of suppressing all attempts of an incipient bourgeoisie to erect a modern capitalist state. What holds of China holds equally truly here of countries like Korea and Vietnam.

Thus capitalism was to China essentially 'foreign', and the more the Chinese saw of it the less they liked it. Even in remote villages people knew of the intense oppression that went on in the industrial parts of the treaty-ports, where capitalism was as un-restrained as it had been before the days of the Factory Acts in Britain. Consequently, in the early days of the Chinese Communist Party in the twenties the question arose, in extremely conscious form, whether it would be possible for modernization and industrialization to be achieved in Chinese culture without passage through all the phases of capitalist development that had occurred in Europe – could they not pass direct to state ownership and socialism? It was decided that they could. Then in 1949 the whole Chinese people gave the answer, a decisive assent. It was a decisive rejection of the Kuomintang Party, which (though originally vaguely revolutionary) had become identified with capitalism, compradors, semi-foreign banks, consortia, conces-sions, the lot. Obviously the historical observer cannot escape the impression that modern socialism has more in common with traditional Chinese bureaucratism than either have with the 'free' entrepreneur and 'free' unprotected labour. The ethos of the party functionary and factory manager has something obviously in common with the non-hereditary magistrate or hydraulic engineer of China's far past – even though the social ideals of a people's democracy are poles apart from those of the traditional imperial bureaucrats.

The idea therefore that capitalism is 'natural' for East Asia is fundamentally false. To propagate it by fire and sword (remem-bering all that that implies in terms of the most horrible of modern war weapon inventions, even short of nuclear devastation) in an East Asian country is therefore an intolerable interference, not only with the natural freedom and self-determination of a people, but with the natural course of development of their own institutions.

Justification of such actions could only take the form of saying that the American way of life is mandatory upon all peoples of the world to adopt. If one does not believe this, then American intervention in Vietnam can only be described as both wicked and immoral, even though the motives of some who support it (as is so often the case, for example with the Holy Inquisition) are doubtless high-minded – Christian liberalism, parliamentary institutionalism, certain concepts of 'freedom', etc.

In all this I short-circuit the involved debates about the juridical status of North and South Vietnam, the international treaties, the laws appealed to by the puppets and propagandists of both sides, all that legalism so much in public dispute at the present time. A third deep misconception of Westerners is that modern international law has a quality of universality which no reasonable man anywhere can call in question. This I think is false, for the kind of law debated at the United Nations has grown up wholly out of Western law, taking no account whatever of the traditions either of Islamic law or of Chinese law. So little are these known that scholars expert in either in the Western world can be numbered on the fingers of the hand. Yet Chinese legal traditions were widely different from those of Roman law or Anglo-Saxon case law; they were averse from codification and devoted to the concrete, with concepts more akin to natural law and equity than to the abstractness of occidental jurisprudence. It is very arguable that Europe (from the sociological if not from the scientific point of view) had much more Euclidean geometry and its counterpart, Roman law, than was good for it. I am not saying that in China law was not, as elsewhere, the principal brake upon inevitable social change, nor that Chinese law was not the instrument of power of the ruling class; what I am saying is that very few Western scholars have paid any attention to it, and that modern international law is far from being truly international, in that its basis is wholly the juristic tradition of the West without any admixture of Asian traditions. Hence perhaps the dominance of the 'legal fiction' so beloved of Westerners. No doubt future historians will select as a prime example of this sinister procedure the determination of America to exclude from the world's counsels the representatives of nearly a quarter of the human race, preferring in their name a group of refugees sitting on an offshore island.

The West thus professes to act in the name of the law. Journalists constantly talk of America as 'the world's policeman'. Asians do not look at matters like this. To them the current mobilization of the self-styled 'free world' seems directed, not so much towards the 'containment of communism' as against the rising upsurge of political consciousness, the national independence movements, and the struggle for industrialization and the raising of living standards to decent minimal levels on the part of those who by a historical accident did not participate in the origins of modern science and the high technology which followed from it.

If then the West is determined to lead the Asian peoples into the path of liberalism and capitalism there is only one truly moral way (compatible with the professions of Christianity) in which this can be done. It is to give financial and technical aid on an infinitely greater scale than has as yet been contemplated – probably greater than ever will be contemplated until it is too late. Capitalism in an agrarian country like Vietnam would have to be demonstrated to have more attractions than the Marxist socialism which has been so successful in China.

Around 1800 the population of the developed countries was about 190 million (twenty-one per cent of the world's population) and they obtained forty-six per cent of the world's income. By 1900 they still represented twenty per cent of the world's population, but acquired fifty-eight per cent of its income. By 1960 we represented thirty-one per cent of the population but our share had risen to eighty-two per cent. In terms of real income people in the developed parts of the world get the equivalent of $970 each per annum, while those in the underdeveloped parts get an average of $95. The corresponding figures for 1800 and 1900 were $200 rising to $400, and $60 rising to $70 respectively. During the past century and a half, therefore, modern technology and its application have greatly increased the disparity between the rich and poor of the world. As has been well said, it does not take an Isaiah or a Jeremiah to see that in the end this must lead to increasing hostility, to wars and rumours of wars, perhaps to an Armageddon of nuclear devastation.

Our own British record of help to underdeveloped countries is extremely poor. France gives some two per cent of the gross national product, Britain not as much as one per cent. Of the £190 million that we give, sixty million goes to Africa, but of this thirty million is in loans, not grants, and twenty million is tied to British products. Only sixteen million is channelled through multilateral or international agencies. Yet in our country alone £900 million is spent each year on betting. As for our position in the international spectrum, it compares poorly with the financial leadership to which London has been accustomed. Of the total aid given by the West in 1963, America supplied sixty per cent, France fourteen per cent and Britain only seven per cent.

It is probable indeed that if the West were to measure up truly to its responsibilities as tutor in capitalism to countries such as Vietnam there would have to be a clearly perceptible fall in the standard of living in countries such as our own. The pips would have to squeak. Though nominally Christian, is there the slightest sign of this self-denying ordinance in Christendom? Could capitalist society in any case do it? Would the working classes willingly accept austerity as the price of aid to the underdeveloped countries? Even if a miracle were to happen, and the wealthy shared this austerity also, would the working classes willingly participate in an effort to induce Asian (and African) peoples to tread the path of capitalism – a system in which they themselves have no real belief, but which they lack the courage and the imagination to change? On such issues anyone's guess is as good as anyone else's.

Yet the alternative is the crime (no kinder word can be used) which is now being perpetrated. I spent some years of my life in the remote parts of China, so that I know what most people in this country do not – the mystique which attaches to factories and railways and two and a half-ton trucks. When you pass through a countryside of river and forest which has never seen a factory chimney, a relatively small fertilizer plant, a methyl alcohol distillery or an electric power station is the most romantic thing in the world. When you can compare a province of three million people which has one single line of railway with one that has not, you know what difference to the modernization of life that communication system with its bridges and tunnels means. When little things like electric torches against poisonous snakes, or rubber boots instead of bare legs, mean so much to those who had to live so long without them, or such banal things as bicycles, what epithet can be used for those who in despicable self-centredness consider themselves fully justified, indeed positively virtuous, in bombing and destroying bridges, factories, work-shops, hospitals, leprosaria, and any place where modern science and technology has raised its head? The systematic destruction of the nascent sprouts of industry and technology in the Korean war was already a perfect example of what is now being repeated in Vietnam. And it does not even work. For it is agreed on all hands that of all the underdeveloped countries North Korea has since the ending of the war there made the greatest strides towards modernization. The Vietnamese will do the same, but they will have little love for the Christendom which is raining down bombs upon them now.

We are living through a terrible period of the misuse of applied science. The Japanese were the first to experience the loathsome effects of an atomic fire-storm. When the news came to Chungking the universal feeling was one of horror, not of relief at the quicker ending of the war ('they would never have done it to a European people') – I know because I was there. First Korean, now Vietnamese, women and children, have been tortured by the indiscriminate use of the liquid fire known as napalm. Scientific ingenuity created, during the Second World War, an astonishing array of engines against fascism, the proximity fuse, shaped plastic explosives, radar detection, phosphorus bombs, nerve gases, rockets, pilotless planes with devastating warheads, mines, etc., etc. Are these, one is inclined to ask, and much more, the technical inventions of the past two decades, now to be used to impose upon the Asian peoples a new fascism, carrying the banner of Christian democracy but without a trace of its true spirit, and designed more than anything else to perpetuate the material supremacy of the white race?

17

YENAN

1964

All places that there are on earth
Can see uniqueness come to birth,
But few there are the world amid
Where actually in fact it did;
Gautama's tree and Newton's chair
Attract all men to homage there,
Winstanley's hill and Lenin's station
Age upon age have veneration.
I found a place of hills and mist
Where loess ravines cascade and twist,
Water of Yen flows brown and thick
The colour of adobe brick,
And oatmeal's eaten; but it's not
The native moorland of the Scot.
It is the province of Shensi
From gross oppression now set free.
Here trod a thinker, a true sage,
A mind appropriate to the age,
Chief of a group that could inspire
To decades of heroic fire;
A man of learning for the people,
A signpost equal to that steeple
That stands aloft on Ching-liang Shan,
To show the right destiny of Man,
A compass for the Kung-chan-tang.
What contrast with the Thien Chu Thang
Built at such cost, to Europe keyed,
To bring to those in direct need,
That which they did not want at all –
But now the Lord of Heaven's Hall
Turns parts for tractors out instead
To help give men their daily bread.

Perhaps the Lord is not offended,
It was, I guess, what he intended.
For all old wisdom is summed up,
Like strongest wine in smallest cup,
In love and brotherhood of man –
But how to incarnate this, who can?
Only a prophet, like Yenan
Saw passing, one who knew
That fundamental nature's true.
Honey will not drive flies away
Nor vinegar induce them stay.
True love means food for every brother.
That is the truth, there is no other.

18

SHAO-SHAN

1964

From the red tilted fields of Devonshire
From the green tarns and black rocks of Merioneth
From the flat skies and deep drains of the Fenland
One awakes from a dream – it is Hunan's red-brown earth.
A homely place, a simple farm, the work of the fields,
What Hesiod sang, and Virgil with piety described;
But here something special, a breath of the Tao itself,
Ling ti, shêng ti, giving birth to a singular man
Who could show the way forward to the Common Life
For seven hundred millions of fellow-men,
Whom all will surely acknowledge their brothers in the end,
As prophesied our Winstanley, and John Ball,
'Once out of time, and your chance is gone';
'In the last day the Trinity shall make all things well'.

Ling: numinous, spiritual. For example, *Ti ling jen chieh*, the place is numinous
and the people gathered there heroic.
Shêng: sagely.

19

PSYCHOLOGY AND SCIENTIFIC
THOUGHT
IN EAST AND WEST

First published in a presentation volume
for Martin Wickramasinghe, 1963

During my stay in Ceylon in the spring and summer of 1958 one
of the things I most enjoyed and appreciated was the opportunity
of getting to know Martin Wickramasinghe, one of the most
outstanding of Lanka's intellectuals, a truly original thinker and
writer in literature and social studies. It was thus a much appreciated honour when I was asked by the editor of this volume to
write something on the books *Buddhist Jātaka Stories and the
Russian Novel*, and *Aspects of Sinhalese Culture*. Although I felt at
first that I had no qualifications for doing so, I reflected that the
birth stories of the Buddha had been known to me from my
student days, for when I was a young man one of the oldest
Fellows of my College in Cambridge was H. T. Francis, the Pali
scholar who made a famous English translation of them. Moreover when I was a Bachelor of Arts at Caius in 1921 and 1922 we
talked of almost nothing else at the B.A.'s Table but psychology,
and especially Freudian psychology, then being introduced widely
to European readers through the explanatory books of A. C.
Tansley.

In his study of the Jātaka stories Wickramasinghe brings out
again and again their relationship to the problems studied in
analytic and introspective psychology of the Freudian era, and
he links this similarity with the surprising resemblances that he
finds in the novels of the great Russian writers of the nineteenth

century. The phenomena of anxiety neurosis, the evil impulses which can arise in man, and the fear of them, the co-existence in proximity in the same mind of the noblest thoughts and the basest urges, all were the common property of the Jātaka authors and the Russian novelists, who long before the clinical fearlessness of modern psychology, shrank from nothing in their determination to inspect everything of which human nature was capable. The Jātaka stories depict a strange and fantastic world of murderers, robbers, tyrants, sexual perverts and courtesans dissatisfied with life and society, but this world has a strong affinity with the world created by Dostoevsky. This is so because both were exploring the subconscious mind, in a pre-scientific but highly impressive manner, the Jātaka writers in the fourth century B.C., the Russians in the nineteenth century A.D. Hence so much of sadism and masochism, in the 'desire for suffering' of Russian fiction. But side by side there is the element of *karuna*, compassion for all living beings.

There may be more concrete historical reasons for the similarity between Russian and Indian–Ceylonese mystical psychology than are mentioned by Wickramasinghe in his book. Those who look upon European civilization from the outside often fail to realize the profound differences between the different forms that Christendom has taken. To say nothing of the churches which arose from the Reformation, the contrast between the Orthodox and the Latin or Roman churches goes very deep. As has so often been said, the Latin priest or theologian took over the mantle of the Roman lawyer, but the Greek priest or patristic writer was the successor of the neo-Platonic philosopher. And thus the Christianity of the Orthodox Churches has always been much more mystical than that of the Latin West. Of course they were also much nearer Asia geographically. This conflict of east and west within Europe was never sharper than in the fourteenth century A.D. when the Hesychasts of the Eastern Churches, led by Gregory Palamas, fought Latin rationalism not only in the interests of a mystical scepticism but to establish methods of meditation very closely resembling the *dhyana* and *samadhi* of yogic and Buddhist discipline, and including the various forms of breathing exercises (*pranayama*) which had also found success far away in the other direction, in Chinese Taoism. Thus the better one is acquainted with some of the influences which have acted upon the Orthodox Churches of Eastern Christendom, the less one is surprised (though the more one admires his perspicacity) to find Wickramasinghe painting Gogol as a *sanyasi* and Father Zosima as a Bodhisattva.

One cannot of course be happy about every one of the notes struck by the Sage of Ambalangoda. I myself confess to feeling uneasy about his kind words addressed to anti-intellectualism. He quotes with approval Gide's remark about Zosima, who has 'reached saintliness by surrender of will and abdication of intellect', and says that all of the saints of the Jātaka stories become so by the rejection of intellect and the extinction of personality. We are told that salvation by suffering is only possible through the crushing of the will and the humiliation of the intellect. Of course everyone knows that *le coeur a ses raisons que la raison ne connait pas*. But surely any purely anti-intellectualist mysticism consorts very oddly with Buddhism, for of all the world's great religions none are more philosophical than this, and unitary though the original doctrine of it was, none have produced greater variety of mutually tolerant schools of interpretation. Surely the nature of the Great Enlightenment was that it 'saw through' the nature of the universe, and so attained the way whereby human suffering could be brought to an end. Everything here is no doubt a matter of emphasis, but among religious systems Buddhism surely can never be reproached with an undervaluation of the intellect, indeed its complex classifications and systematizations quite rival the scholasticism of the Latin West. Certainly as a historian of science I have long delighted to recognize the very advanced character of medieval Buddhist speculation about the universe. With its imaginative belief in the existence of millions of beings in a single drop of water, or millions of universes in each grain of sand, it was far more in key with the nature of the universe as modern science has revealed it than were the cosmological conceptions of ancient and medieval Europe. Like the Chinese astronomers, medieval Buddhists imagined the stars as objects of unknown nature floating in infinite empty space. Their universe was a far more open one than that of medieval Western Europeans, imprisoned as they were within the concentric eggshells of the crystalline celestial spheres – paradoxically the product of that Euclidean geometry and Ptolemaic planetary astronomy which were the forerunners of modern science itself, at any rate in large part. Monks enquired of a Bodhisattva how long it would take for a stone thrown from the *Tusita* heaven to reach *Jambu-dvipa*, the earth, and the answer was in terms of millions of years – 'light-years', as we should say nowadays. This was in a fabricated sūtra, but in real life the same difference was apparent, for when about A.D. 720 the great Tantric astronomer I-Hsing in China computed the date of the first general conjunction he made it come out to something like 97,000,000 years before his time. Yet 900 years later in England, a dignitary of another religion, James Usher, Archbishop of Armagh, was seriously calculating the date of creation as October 22, 4004 B.C. at six o'clock in the evening.

Usher was no anti-intellectualist, but not a few Westerners were. As I write this in the midst of the beautiful countryside of France I think of St Bernard of Clairvaux and his *cultus ignorantiae*, as well as the Orthodox Hesychasts of the Aegean shores. Buddhism may have had its anti-intellectual mystics but as a whole the anti-intellectualist label will not stick on it.

Indeed I believe that when in time to come the contributions of Indian and Buddhist thought are really taken in hand from the point of view of the natural sciences, it will be found over and over again that the philosophers of this culture-area shot their arrows correctly to the spots that the mountaineers of science would reach definitively much later on. A good deal of work has already been done in this connection, but all of it will have to be revised and reconsidered, partly because we still do not possess an adequate chronological framework for Indian texts, and partly because we still need theoretical studies in the philosophy of science to lay down criteria and say just what it means to assert that a particular ancient philosophical system developed concepts closely analogous to those of the modern natural sciences. An example lies immediately to hand. Martin Wickramasinghe points out that the evil impulses, murderous thoughts, suicidal tendencies, etc. in the characters of the Jātaka corpus were all accounted for by its writers in terms of the doctrine of *karma*, or 'spiritual heritage', man's feelings and instincts being considered the accumulated inheritance from the former bundles of *skandhas* connected with him, or (in popular Buddhist thought) 'his' own previous lives. Wickramasinghe suggests that the theory of *karma* was what led the Buddhist fabulists to their proto-psychoanalytic approach, and intimates that it was not so far wrong after all since modern science has recognized the existence of atavistic tendencies arising from the animal past of mankind. Thus the unplumbed depths of human psychological constitution contain still much of the beast, much of the most primitive ape-man, and in so far as *karma* meant this atavistic load still present from the past it was a fair anticipation of a valid scientific idea arising from our modern knowledge of organic evolution.

How far it may be justified to admit this anticipation I am not quite sure, but I think it is so to some degree. Elsewhere (in his *Aspects of Sinhalese Culture*) Wickramasinghe has drawn attention to the Vedantic and Ayurvedic theory of *koshas* or envelopes. There is an envelope of chemical matter, an envelope of life, an envelope of mind, an envelope of consciousness, and an envelope of bliss or soul. The idea of this was that the world was like a series of onion skins or sheaths, and by stripping these off one by one it was possible to reach the inmost essential being of man and of nature. Wickramasinghe likens these ideas to the modern scientific conception of spatial envelopes: the electron is in the atom, the atom in the molecule, the molecule in the colloidal particle, the particle in the organelle, the organelle in the cell, the cell in the organ, the organ in the body, the body in the social unit, etc. We find the same thought again in a Taoist writer of the eighth century A.D., Wang Shih-Yuan, who in his *Khang Tshang Tzu* has a theory of 'disrobing'. When earth (element) disrobes, we find only water (element), when water 'moults' or 'disrobes' there is nothing left but empty *chhi* (more or less equivalent to *pneuma* or *prana*), then that in turn unveils itself as naked Emptiness (*hsü*), and after one last disembodiment we come face to face with the Tao (the Order of Nature, somewhat equivalent to *Rta*). In all these questions we have to steer a careful course between the tendency to attribute too much to the formulations of the ancient and medieval thinkers, and the opposite tendency to write them all off as speculative dreamers without contact with reality as modern science has revealed it to us. It will take decades of work before we can state precisely how far the ancient and medieval thinkers intuitively penetrated the secrets of the natural world and formulated them in their own ways.

In my work on the Neo-Confucian philosophical school (eleventh to thirteenth centuries A.D.) I have shown in considerable detail that without the advantage of post-Renaissance experimental science, Chu Hsi and his friends succeeded in reducing the natural world to precisely the two fundamental entities which modern science has arrived at – Matter-energy and Organization, or, in the medieval Chinese terms, *chhi* and *li*. I am sure that similarly profound conceptions will be recognizable in some of the Indian philosophies, for example the Samkhya. As Kovur Behanan has shown, the element of perpetual change in the universe may be recognized in *rajas*, while the persistence of particular patterns, inertia and the conservation of mass, was what was meant by *tamas*. The third of the three *gunas*, *sattva*, intelligence or mind-stuff, was considered a perfectly natural development, arising out of matter when the organizational level became sufficiently complicated, and was thought of as that which had the conscious power to gain knowledge and experience. As Chu Hsi was later to say: 'Cognition (or apprehension) is the essential pattern of the mind's existence, but that there is (something in the world) which can do this, is (what we may call) the spirituality inherent in matter.' Neither for Samkhya nor for Taoism, both systems beginning in the third or fourth century B.C., was there any room for supernaturalism in the strict sense.

These considerations are brought forward to offer support for Martin Wickramasinghe's admirable efforts to validate and comprehend the ancient philosophical systems of the Indo–Ceylonese culture-area, and at the same time to criticize his slight penchant for anti-intellectualism. My belief is that Indo–Ceylonese culture as a whole has been fundamentally misunderstood by historians of thought in the East as well as the West. The indubitable prevalence and indeed dominance of religious feeling and metaphysical idealism has been allowed to overshadow far too seriously the very real and widespread elements of naturalism and materialism. Thanks to scholars such as Debiprasad Chattopadhyaya, with his excellent study of Lokayata doctrines, there is a beginning now being made to redress this balance. The study of the history of science and technology in Chinese culture is bringing to light an extraordinary wealth of discoveries and inventions which passed to the West and were often accepted there without any clear knowledge of where they had come from, but the scientific thought of China travelled less because the linguistic difficulties were too great for its transmission. By and large one must also say that it fell short of the deductive geometry and the formal logic of the Greeks. We cannot forejudge what the future developments of the history of science will bring forth, but if India was probably less original than China in the engineering and physico-chemical sciences, Indian culture in all probability excelled in systematic thought about Nature (as for example in the Samkhya atomic theories of *kshana*, *bhutadi*, *paramanu*, etc.), including also biological speculations.

It is for these reasons that I believe a famous thesis of the American scholar F. S. C. Northrop, to be deeply mistaken. In his book *The Meeting of East and West* Northrop maintained that a fundamental difference in apprehension of reality divided Asia from Europe. The basis of Eastern culture was said to be intuitive and aesthetic, that of Western culture experimental and scientific. While in one place (*Buddhist Jātaka Stories and the Russian Novel*, p. 64) Wickramasinghe seems to smile upon this opinion, in another (p. 129) however, he more thoroughly opposes it, urging that both in East and West there have been materialist and scientific currents just as there have been religious and idealist ones. Before I began my own work I had a fairly open mind on this subject, but all that I have since learned seems to contradict the Northrop theory. In all the civilizations there were tendencies both scientific and anti-scientific. Which of them dominate at particular times and places seems to me now to depend far more upon the social and economic structure of the culture than upon any supposed racial penchants for one world-outlook or another. In the West there was first the free-flying speculation of the Greeks, but it was followed by the 'dark ages' of feudalism (the term is not entirely wrong, greatly criticized though it has been), and a tremendous effort had to be made to bring about the breakthrough of the Renaissance in which modern science was born. In China there was not the Hellenic upsurge but there was not the medieval hibernation period either, and for the first fourteen centuries Chinese culture was in most ways ahead, and often unbelievably far ahead, of any science which Europe could show. But no Renaissance followed, for Chinese feudal-bureaucratic society was much more stable than the feudalism of Europe. The intellectual history of India and Ceylon remains to be analysed, but it looks as if those societies were no more favourable to naturalist philosophy and scientific advance than that of China, indeed very probably much less so, with the result that speculation alone could flourish, and often not even that. Nevertheless when the balance comes to be made up, it will be found, I believe, that Indian scientific history holds as many brilliant surprises as those which have emerged from the recent study of China – whether in mathematics, chemistry, or biology, and especially the theories which were framed about them.

With this thought I offer my salutations to the Sage of Ambalangoda – just such a thought as one might discuss sitting in the evening before the door of the philosopher's home, and looking across the Ceylonese countryside as the sun sets in the west.

20

THE PILGRIM COMES AGAIN
TO CHHIEN-FO-TUNG

1958

Near Tunhuang in Kansu, a few miles away from the Old Silk Road, lie
• the famous cave-temples of Chhien-fo-tung (the Thousand Buddha Caves) or
Mo-kao-khu. As Yün-kang, with its wealth of carvings and sculptures, corresponds to Ellora in India, so Chhien-fo-tung corresponds to Ajanta. About
350 caves, ranging in size from a suit-case to a cathedral, and running along the
southern face of a sharp escarpment beside a wooded oasis on the edge of a dry
river-bed, are full of fresco-paintings of the utmost beauty and magnificence.
This Buddhist settlement was founded by the monk Lo-Tsun in A.D. 366,
and got its first abbot a little later in Fa-Lang. The peace, the remoteness and
the loveliness of the place makes it the Mount Athos of Central Asia. The
oldest extant works of art there date from c. A.D. 450, and the last caves were
excavated and ornamented in the fourteenth century A.D.

Fifteen hundred years ago in a bad time
Hideous with strife of the warlords of the Chin
There came the first of the monks to Mo-kao-khu
Hid in its little oasis in the San-Wei Shan
And seeing the red-gold Buddha-light on the evening hills
Knew that the place was blessed and benign
And hollowed a cave to chant his liturgy.

Century after century followed on,
Cave after cave was limned and sanctified,
Monk after monk lived out his regular days,
Elegant in Thang and learned in the Sung,
Weighing with open mind the deep philosophy
Of god and *shakti* Yuan lamas brought,
Or in the Ming with *chhan* adepts discoursing
On stranger paths of paradox and void –

And one yet sits gazing across to his tower
And one on painted wall perpetual incense burns
And others' ashes rest in the desert stupa-tombs
With their coloured plaster polished and scoured like bone
By the howling sandstorms of a thousand autumns.

These monks did homage to the ideal of love,
Tathagata's love for all existing things,
And sacrifice of self they understood,
And lived the common life that love defines.
Part of the truth they had, but missed the clue,
For not by flight from the world of men's desires
Can man's salvation be attained on earth –
Only by understanding of his history
Only by finding the laws of social life
Can that true alchemy perform its work
Transmute all want to right harmonious will
And love be incarnate in man's polity.

And here at the heart of the world was a meeting-place
Where from the Old Silk Road the wayfaring men
Offering vows and incense turned aside.
The crafty Sogdian merchants always came
(For well does it pay to please the desert gods)
And Persians bearing the night-shining jewel,
And Jewish Rhadanites from far Provence
Carrying Roman glass and sea-sheep bags –
And always westbound went the bales of silk
In Chinese convoy to the Old Stone Tower.
So while the camp-fires died at Chhien-fo-tung
The talk turned often to the West and East
And all their manifold diversity
Of Magian lore and subtile Indian thought
Of Hebrew Turks and Christian Aethiops
Of acrobats and strange mechanick arts –
Whence on the painted walls we see today
Greek fauns supporting Tantric ecstasies
And all the signs of the Western zodiac dance
Round Sakyamuni's bright triumphal car.

Craftsmen innumerable gathered too
Stumbling across the sands with their paints and brush
Masters of drawing, free of colour and line.
Buddhas and Bodhisattvas blossomed fair
Yet their delight was in all common things,
Harness and plough, milling and winnowing,
Faring and ship-faring, masonry and forge;
Set in the legends of Gautama's lives
But telling for ever of life in the Sui and Thang
And how the ancestors lived in China of old.

Fifteen years ago in a bad time
In a world groaning and travailing with the fascist ill,
It was my lot to come first to this dear place
(Half scientist, half humanist *Han-hsüeh chia*,
The spirit of Galileo in the blood
But also a learner in Ssuma Chhien's school)
With a New Zealand friend, the best of friends,
Two Kansu boys, and a Chinese painter from Paris
Braving the desert and steppe with his beret so gay.
Here marooned for weeks with a broken engine –
Good fortune enough and to spare it was.
Of comfort little but of beauty abundance,
Short of provisions but in delight most rich –
Washing our clothes in the stream from the Han fort,
Gathering mushrooms for soup from the sandy edges,
Munching Yi Lama's *thieh-tzu* in the middle temple,
Happiness, purest happiness was ours.
Waking in the night we heard the iron horses
Jangling their lauds in the desert breeze,
A sound to remain in the heart as long as life lasts.
The trees bending under the wind we loved
The water running in its sandy channels
The caves each one more beautiful than the next
(With a shock now and then from Wang Tao-shih's glass eyes)
Apsaras adorable sweeping through the air
Delicious daughters of Mara, surely never evil,
And the furious winds of the Northern Wei
That blow down the devils of the later Thang –
'Blow the man down' they sang, like the English chanty.

And one could trudge across to the San-Wei Shan,
Up to Wang's phai-lou – 'Ni lai liao ma?'
And follow the rocky road to Kuan-Yin Ching
And climb to the five Han beacons of the long-lost outpost
And be shadowed by wolves, and go in fear of the Khazaks.
But lonely, lonely it was.
Yi Lama said: 'Yes, the leaves are falling,
And men are falling, too.
Soon there will be no-one left
At Chhien-fo-tung.'

Now in a year of grace, and my year, fifty-eight,
I come again to the temples in the sands,
With an old friend, my evocator and expounder,
Opener of the doors of division, my welcomer,
And new friends bearing the future in themselves,
And our driver with the face of a Han commander
Harrying the Huns beyond the Great Wall.
From Angkor, Anurādhapura too
In Fa-Hsien's footsteps treading I have passed,
Like him come home, but finding home all radiant
With novel strength and inexhaustible life.
At Chhien-fo-tung men have arisen anew
And Yi himself still living, happy to hear
The cries of children echoing through the groves.
Devoted archaeologists preserve
Those treasures which lay naked for so long,
Prey for all bandits, vandals and misuse.
And far across the desert after dawn
The solitary walker hears Mo-Kao's bells
Ring as in ancient days they used to do,
Marking the common life, but now in affirmation lived,
No longer in denial, of human things.

So I depart, not lacking every hope
That fate will lead me back yet once, yet once,
To eat with Pipit behind the screen
The bread of durable peace at the heart of the world.

San-Wei Shan: Mountains of the Three Dangers, a low desert range across the valley from Chhien-fo-tung.

Shakti: energizing female consorts of gods in Hinduism and Tantric Buddhism.

Chhan: Zen Buddhism.

Han-hsüeh chia: sinologist.

Thieh-tzu: a remarkable fruit that grows at Chhien-fo-tung, in shape like an apple, in integument like a pear, as also in the texture of the flesh, but in taste like a quince, though very sweet.

Iron horses: *thich ma,* Aeolian bells hung at the corners and along the edges of temple roofs.

Wang Tao-shih: the Taoist Wang, in charge of the temples at the time of the celebrated visits of Aurel Stein and Paul Pelliot, who conveyed away the greater part of the manuscript library to London and Paris. Wang, it is said, sold the library with the intention, pious as it seemed to him, of restoring as many as possible of the damaged caves, and some of this he did, but the artistic standards attainable in his time were atrocious, hence the startling glass eyes of some of the figures he put up.

Apsaras: Buddhist angels, very prominent at Chhien-fo-tung.

Phai-lou: triumphal gateway of wood and tile. On the way over the barren hills to an isolated temple by a well sacred to Kuan-Yin, the Goddess of Mercy, and at an extremely lonely place, Wang Tao-shih had set up one of these, with the inscription: 'What! Have *you* come here?'

Beacons: this place was on the defence lines of the Han empire, so that besides forts there were small truncated pyramids in groups of five, used in ancient times for signalling.

Khazaks: one of the tribal peoples of Sinkiang, at that time very much on the rampage in north-western Kansu.

SCIENCE AND RELIGION
IN THE LIGHT OF ASIA

Speech given at a Cambridge Union
Society debate on 9 May, 1961 in reply
to the motion 'Where Science Advances,
Religion Recedes'

The Hon. Proposers of this motion have clearly demonstrated that
the conventional institutional popular Christianity of the western
world is subject to the dissolving power of the scientific view of
the universe. More and more, as mankind succeeds in penetrating
the secrets of Nature, naive religious beliefs must succumb; the
doctrinal certainties of the past are transmuted into a corpus of
legend, the essential truths of liturgy find explanation and re-
statement in new terms, and slowly but surely the practice of even
the most orthodox groups changes as the generations pass. The
advance of science must necessarily lead to the increasing puri-
fication of religious philosophy, and to new interpretations of
theology; with a corresponding disappearance of popular religious
folklore to join the flat earth and the underground hell in the
limbo of the past. Yet I find myself on the opposition side because
the terms of the motion say that *religion* as such recedes as science
advances, and that is a very different matter.

Religion, the distinctive sense of the holy, the appreciation of
the category of the numinous, attached as it has been in its most
developed forms to the highest ethical principles known to man,
altogether transcends the particular manifestations of it familiar
in our parochial and limited experience. I believe that we can only

consider this motion rightly if we try to take into consideration all the religious experiences of mankind, including the great systems of Asia, still very much alive. We must be ecumenical and catholic (with small letters, not capitals). We must take off the swaddling clothes of the Christmas carol mentality in which most of us have grown up, and see what religion as such really means to the world, not only fragments of medieval Latin theology garbled into English and popularly misconceived. If science is and will be universal, so religion is and will continue to be.

For religion does not necessarily imply a doctrine of a creator god at all. The ideas of this House about it might have been very much influenced if, like myself, its members had spent a considerable amount of time in Confucian temples. The doctrine of the sage, Khung Chung-Ni (Khung Fu-Tzu) was fundamentally a this-worldly social ethic; he claimed to have found the way of forbearance, sacrifice and love, whereby men and women could live together in harmony and happiness all the days of their life. To this doctrine in the most fundamental sense the 'myriad black-haired people' (the Chinese) have been faithful from the sixth century B.C. right down to the present day. Confucius himself did not deny the existence of gods and spirits, he only advised keeping them at a distance and having as little to do with them as possible. 'You do not yet know how to serve your fellow-men; how should I teach you how to serve spirits?' And though Confucianism was established as an official cult from the Han dynasty onwards, sacerdotalism never found a place in it. The beautiful Confucian temples, scattered over the length and breadth of the Chinese culture-area in every town however small, saw liturgical observances only once a year, on the sage's birthday, and then the celebrant was the provincial governor or the local magistrate, assisted by all the civil servants of lower rank – for Confucianism had become the characteristic faith of the mandarinate. The rest of the time the temple housed a library frequented by the local scholars, a school of the traditional kind, and other public institutions – for Confucius had been a revolutionary in his belief that everyone who could profit by education should receive it, altogether irrespective of birth or status. Fundamentalist Christians in their spiritual pride (perhaps the greatest of human sins – to adopt their own conceptions) no doubt wrote off all this as mere heathenism. But I can testify from personal experience that I have nowhere felt the presence of the numinous more strongly than in Confucian temples where, in the main hall, there are rarely any images, only behind the altar a great tablet of sculptured wood in its shrine, with characters written on it which read: 'The perfumed throne of the perfected sage, Confucius, teacher of ten thousand generations.' And all around stand the smaller wooden tablets bearing the name of his 166 canonized disciples.

Ancient Chinese religion laid much emphasis on rite and liturgy, but the great Confucian tradition was that it was more important for the participants than for the ancestral or other spirits to whom the sacrifice was being made. This interpretation of sacramental acts in psychological rather than theological terms goes back far into the history of Chinese thought. I should like to read a few words from the *Li Chi* (The Record of Rites) compiled about 50 B.C. but containing material from times back to the beginning of the fifth century B.C.

All living creatures inevitably come to die. Dying, they inevitably go back to the earth. This is what is meant by the 'material soul' (*kuei*). The bones and flesh moulder below, and hidden there, make the soil of the land. But the spirit (*chhi*) soars aloft to become light, and is found in the fragrance and the feeling of sorrow at the sacrifice. Here then is the refined essence of the hundred kinds of creatures; here is the manifestation of the spiritual soul (*shen*) in man.

The conception of liturgy as mystically instructive and profoundly beneficial poetry is thus by no means an invention of our time. Elsewhere the *Li Chi* says:

There should be no repetitions of a sacrifice, for that would be importunity, and hence irreverence. Neither should a sacrifice be at too infrequent intervals, for that would be indifference, and hence a forgetting of the holy ancestors. Thus it is that a man of refinement, being in harmony with the Tao of Heaven, offers the autumn and the spring sacrifices to the dead. For when the hoar-frost is on the ground, as he treads on it, he is sure to be conscious of a sadness which is nothing to do with his being cold, but with those he loved being

parted from him by cold death. Then when the spring rains and dews fall, as
he treads on the springing grass, he is sure to have a feeling of excitement, as if he
were soon to see them. And since guests are escorted with sorrow when they
depart, and welcomed with music when they come again, so the autumn sacrifice
is silent, but at the spring sacrifice there is sound of voice and instrument.

How should religion such as this recede when science makes
advance? So long as man remains man, experiencing a lifting of
the heart at sight of an apple-tree in blossom, or at the passing of
a girl in the flower of her youth, so long as he continues to appreciate the meanings of songs and poems, he will feel a need for
the recognition of the numinous too, and its embodiment in corporate observance and rite. In this there is nothing inconsistent
with the appreciation of the scientific sense of the role of chance
in natural phenomena. And not only nothing now, but nothing
(for a Chinese scholar) in the first century A.D. either. We can
all enjoy the story of Liu Khun, as the *Hou Han Shu* tells it.

When Liu Khun was prefect of Chiang-ling, his city was devastated by fire.
But he prostrated himself before it, and it immediately went out. Later, when
he became prefect of Hungnung, the tigers (which had previously infested the
place) swam across the Yellow River with their cubs on their backs and
migrated elsewhere. The emperor heard about these things and wondered at
them, and promoted Liu Khun Chief of the Personnel Department. The
emperor said to him: 'Formerly, at Chiang-ling you turned back the wind and
extinguished the conflagration, and then at Hungnung you sent the tigers north
of the river; by what virtue did you thus manage affairs?' Liu Khun replied:
'It was all pure chance.' The courtiers to left and right could not restrain their
smiles (to see a man losing such a fine opportunity of getting on in the world).
But the emperor said: 'This reply is worthy of a really superior man. Let the
annalists record it.'

Thus men like Liu Khun, though rationalists to the core, believed
also in the benefit of rite and liturgy (even as in this case exorcistic)
as the most perfect expressions of the emotion of the human
community. Perhaps the world has hardly yet begun to learn
from Confucian wisdom. Yet if you visit China today, you will
find the Confucian temples restored to their former glories at
the expense of public funds, and if you read the speeches of

contemporary Chinese leaders you will find them quoting from the Confucian classics.

In another of the great religions of Asia, Buddhism, once again we find no theology of a creator god, or any other kind of supreme deity, no insistence on miracles daily renewed, no priesthood and no claim to infallibility. Here eschatology is automatic. The Lord Buddha (as I learnt to call him in Ceylon), no less historical than Confucius, was again not a god but a man, though gifted with supreme, almost 'divine', penetration into the order of Nature. He believed he could see working therein a kind of law as unerring as the law of gravity, the law that the sins of the fathers would be visited upon the children unto the thirtieth and fortieth generation, but that by right conduct and right thought these sins could be avoided, so that the individual instead of being by the natural process condemned to live on through life after life of earthly sorrow, could escape from the wheel of existence. By cultivating compassion (*karuna*) for all beings, he could at last enter the paradise of nescience (*nirvana*). Here the numinous is again most deeply associated with ethical insights, and the salvation, though in a way personal, is primarily *from* self. Self-restraint, self-control, self-sacrifice, is seen, as in Confucianism, to be the clue to human solidarity and social order, though the goal of Buddhism is the 'ferrying over to the other shore', while Confucius' disciples recognize no other than this. About the status of Confucianism as a religion some may wonder, but no one will have any doubts about Buddhism, whether in its pure and primitive southern Hinayana form, or in its 'catholic' northern Mahāyāna manifestation. Again from personal experience in Buddhist temples – Lankatillaka, Gadaladeniya, Abhayagiriya, Mihintale – evocatively beautiful Sinhalese names – or in China at Hua-Thing Ssu or on Chin-Yün Shan no less – not the most exquisite cathedral of all Christendom can inspire in the visitor and the worshipper a more profound sense of the numinous. How will the advance of science affect this religion? The mythological system and even the belief in reincarnation may crumble, but the liberation of the self by the practice of compassion, with all its psychological justification, will remain, and hence the worship of the Enlightened One. Buddhists too can take legitimate pride in pointing out that their conceptions of natural law anticipated those of the Stoics and the Renaissance scientists by many centuries, and it is undeniably true that the medieval Buddhist conception of the universe, with its almost infinite spaces, was more sophisticated and enlightened than the closed prison of the crystalline celestial spheres which surrounded medieval Christendom.[1] Indeed, for Buddhism as for the Confucians there is really no realm of the 'supernatural' at all, in spite of the rather alarming appearances of Hindu and other deities enlisted as 'protectors of the faith'. They are only beings on a higher level of existence, and just as much in need of salvation as men are, or any other living beings. Thus in Ceylon, for instance, the people pray to Vishnu, as if to St Anthony, to help them find lost rings or watches – but as for salvation (from self) that is quite another matter.

Who shall set bounds to natural knowledge, or declare the limits of what human science, that social structure so long in the building, may attain? The successive levels of organization in the universe will always require their separate approaches, but understanding of the relations between the levels will grow more and more. Neuro-physiology, experimental psychology and the bio-chemistry of the brain will some day elucidate the functioning of our mental and spiritual life. I rejoice at this prospect, but I remember that knowledge will bring power and control. If, as we hope and believe, this developed science will banish for ever the terrors of mental disease which have plagued humanity so long, it will bring also all kinds of unheard-of possibilities of biological engineering – as every scientific advance must do. How then, and for what purpose will these be used? Like fire itself, like atomic energy, all such powers may be employed for evil or for good, and the problem of what kind of society men have, with what ideals and what protections, becomes not less important but ever more and more so. Many in this House will share my conviction that only a socialist form of society will ensure that science

[1] Cf. p. 179.

is used for human benefit rather than human destruction. Perhaps several centuries hence the chief meaning of the term democracy will be seen to lie in the question whether or not science is applied primarily *for people*. 'Science for science's sake' seems only too often to cloak the idea of 'science for the sake of big profits' or 'science for the sake of defence' (i.e. the piling up of armaments). At any rate the supporters of the first notion rarely seem to criticize the second or the third. It may be true that science cannot flourish in a stifling atmosphere of government control, but under private corporate enterprise its utilization primarily for the benefit of the people as a whole seems often far from obvious. To leaf over the advertisement pages of what is perhaps the greatest journal of popular science in the world, the *Scientific American*, is a veritable nightmare. Science for war is dominant: 'automatic accurate attack', 'electronic equipment for missile launching', 'skybolt deterrent', 'heat shields for ICBM nose-cones'. Calculating machines, rocket propulsion, orbiting satellites, cybernetic devices, substances injurious to plants and animals, new drugs, cloud-seeding, subliminal instruction – for what, for what? We are now invited to throw religious sanctions out of the window; we had better be careful that this does not end in kicking ethics downstairs. For ethics and the appreciation of the numinous are intimately and inextricably associated. I boldly conclude therefore that a thousand years hence (if mankind has not been blotted out), the sense of the holy will still exist in the full man, as it has from the beginning, along with his other fundamental activities, aesthetic experience, historical perception, and the ratiocination of philosophy and science. And it will be applied, just as the Chinese of old applied it, to the sacrifices of the culture-heroes of the past (and of the future), in veneration of all those who have worked and died that justice and knowledge, love and comradeship, might flourish on the earth.

The Hon. Proposer referred, as expected, to religion as the 'opium of the people' (or if he did not, it was by an oversight). Of course in its other-worldly and established forms it has been this, throughout human history, both in East and West, but that is not the whole state of the case. We are quite ready to quote the Lucretian words *tantum religio potuit suadere malorum* when we hear how the Aztecs butchered hundreds of thousands in human sacrifice for fear that the sun and planets would not continue on their courses; we are not so ready to take them to heart when we read of the Crusades and pogroms against Muslims, Jews and Albigensians, still less so when we learn of the family miseries caused by rigid ecclesiastical prohibitions, whether Latin or Puritan, or when we listen to the clergy preaching personal salvation instead of social regeneration. 'True religion and undefiled before God' there has always been, and some of the greatest atheists and agnostics have demonstrated it, to say nothing of the mystics such as William Blake. Thirty years ago I wrote: 'Not to be awake to the iniquity of class oppression, that is religious "opium".' But I added that there was something we might call 'scientific hashish' as well. Not to be awake to the tragic side of life, and to the numinous element in the world, and of human effort towards righteousness in the world, was how I thought of it, but today it seems to me far more dangerous than in the pre-atomic age. Scientists who, dismissing religious and even philosophical experience as nonsense, think only of cultivating their talents as mathematical physicists or experimental biologists to the utmost, and training others to follow them in this, while refusing to make any judgments within the political field, and ignoring what the society in which they live does with their discoveries, are truly in danger of becoming 'hashishin', assassins (for this is the derivation of the word), the destroyers of the innocent on a scale infinitely exceeding Herod. Let us beware, therefore, of making too much play with the idea of 'opium of the people'; today the 'hashish of the scientists' is becoming a danger quite as great.

In what I have been saying so far I have had in mind religion as the sense of the numinous applied to the highest ethical values. The Hon. Proposer will certainly agree that this plays a fundamental part in the motivation of socialist and communist movements, and if, as he would assert, they are inevitably fore-ordained by the intrinsic logic of history, is that not because man is made as he is? Few would deny the element of the numinous in the tomb of Lenin in the Red Square, as in many other observances in the socialist world, so that even if the visible church should pass away, as Buddhists say it was prophesied that the *sangha* shall, religion will be reincarnated in forms ever new. Meanwhile there are at least some Christians who celebrate in the eucharist the memory of all those who gave their lives for truth, united with him who is for them the supreme embodiment of sacrifice.

This brings us at last to the fact that there is also the worship of the 'greater than ourselves', the 'mysterium tremendum', the 'wholly other'. For certain minds at least it remains exactly as true as it was in the eighteenth century that the more a man knows of astronomy and cosmology the more infinitely small he feels, and by the same token the more infinitely worthy of adoration is the power or pattern 'behind the universe'. It need not be personal in any sense that we can conceive; let us first think of it as immanent. I believe that from the theological point of view the stirring controversies among radio-astronomers in which the Hon. Seconder has recently been involved were of much less import than often supposed, for a steady-state universe was not at all unknown to deist philosophy. In the seventeenth- and eighteenth-century doctrine of the General Concourse, it was thought necessary that God should perpetually uphold the universe to prevent it degenerating into chaos again. So also, long before, there had been the attractive thinker Hermogenes, who pictured God as a field of magnetic force holding all things and processes together. We have said something of the Confucians already, but there was another ancient Chinese school, one which passed beyond the ethics of human society to venerate the immanent power – I mean of course the Taoists; for whom the Tao, 'the Unvarying Way, and not the way that can be talked about', was the Order of Nature. In their temples also have I passed many hours, with infinite profit. I remember the beautiful shrine of Hei-lung Than (the Black Dragon Pool) near Kunming, where in the lower halls you might find images of the bureaucrats in the

Taoist pantheon, fit godlings for an old-style peasant to honour with an incense-stick – but when one came to the uppermost hall on the hillside there one found nothing but emptiness, save a single great carved inscription behind the altar – *Wan Wu chih Mu* – Nature, the mother of all things. My belief is that men will never cease to want to practise this religion, this basic piety towards the universe into which they are born.

As for us Westerners, our theological inheritance is in many ways unpropitious compared with those of our Asian friends. Of course I do not mean to say that their religious systems were any freer than ours in practice from superstition, hypocrisy, and slavery to established orders of society. But how strange is the paradox that in that very part of the world which alone gave rise to modern (as distinguished from ancient and medieval) science, religion should have generated so much indefensible theology in the service of the uncompromisingly transcendental and the irreconcilably tragic. Fanaticism has not been confined to Christendom, but we have had rather more than our fair share of it. Greek philosophy was pressed into the service of orthodoxy to refine the details of a mountain of dogma; Roman law was conscripted to safeguard an organization whose pontifex was far more maximal and supreme than any priest of antiquity. As time went on, idealist and subjectivist philosophies, familiar to the Indians but never popular in China, added their support to the anti-scientific attitudes always so easily induced by the Church, which gave way unwillingly and step by step. Nevertheless, mistaken though it has often been, and unfavourably though we may sometimes be moved to compare it with certain Asian religions, our religion it was. I therefore maintain that no European who wishes to retain contact with his own heritage and traditions (hoping indeed perhaps thereby to enter in with greater sympathy to those of other cultures) can afford to cut himself off from active experience of one or other of the great forms which religion has taken in his own civilization. He may well prefer not to strain his sense of the reasonable too much, and if so that religion which he professes will not recede as science advances, for any religion truly so called can never do so. All superstition will be swept away, all false theology will disappear, but the holiness of 'mercy, pity, peace and love' will remain. Indeed they and they alone will be able to save science from the utter disasters which otherwise the misuse of it will bring upon mankind.

22

CHRISTIANITY
AND THE ASIAN CULTURES

Sermon preached in Gonville and Caius
College Chapel, on 22 January, 1961

In the name of God the compassionate, the merciful.

There was no difficulty about choosing one of those devices with which sermons begin. At the celebration of the Liturgy on the first Sunday of the present university year the Epistle said:

There is one body and one spirit, even as ye are called in one hope of your calling; one Lord, one faith, one baptism, one God and Father of all, who is above all and through all and in us all.

And the Gospel was read as follows:

And when thou art bidden to a wedding, go and sit down in the lowest room; so that when he that bade thee cometh he may say unto thee, 'Friend, go up higher.' For whosoever exalteth himself shall be abased; and he that humbleth himself shall be exalted.

And this morning we heard it said:

And many shall come from the east and the west and shall sit down with Abraham and Isaac and Jacob in the kingdom of heaven.

Surely these are great statements of the unity of humanity, and of the true humility which all individual groups of humanity should have. Humility is surely only a concealed form of love, a willingness to give to the 'others' the benefit of the doubt, to be prepared to learn from them, and in short a refusal to say that 'we are the people' and that 'wisdom was born with us'. Unfortunately, looking round upon the whole Western world at the present time, there is not much sign of this humility – more perhaps than there was, but still far from enough. Western civilization is still suffering from an unjustifiable cultural pride which vitiates all its contacts with the other peoples of the world; this may truly be called 'spiritual wickedness in high places', and also τὰ πνευματικὰ τῆς πονηρίας ἐν τοῖς ἐπουρανίοις – the 'spirit of evil in things heavenly'.

Christians today are called, I believe, to re-think their entire position with regard to the other great civilizations and religions of the world. For social evolution does not stand still; we are no longer living in Origen's time, no longer in the days of Thomas of Aquino, nor even of John Wesley – immeasurable advances have been made not only in knowledge of Nature but also of other lands and other cultures of living brothers and sisters to us, unknown in the old time or totally misunderstood. The difficulty of regarding oneself as the repository of a timeless truth is that one so easily fails to recognize it in the new forms which it comes to take; for the Holy Spirit makes all things new.

Perhaps the two most breathtaking processes which have led to our present situation are the rise of modern science in Europe from the beginning of the seventeenth century onwards and the renaissance of Asia from the beginning of the twentieth. The birth of modern, as distinct from ancient and medieval, science, was simply the complete discovery of the method of discovery itself. Only three years before John Caius was laid to rest here beside us, Galileo was born, the greatest of all the founders of modern science with the possible exception of Newton, so that Caius stood on the very threshold of the new age. What connection the Christian religion had with this great break with the past (if any) is a complicated question into which we have no time to enter this evening, but whatever it was it was certainly no more important than the social and economic conditions which favorized the development of modern science in Western Europe, and nowhere else on the earth's surface. That modern science was a Pandora's

Box is fairly widely appreciated today; everything modern, good and bad, came out of it, but I should like to show you something very bad, which was quite different from the present-day dilemma of international morals in the age of atomic fission and fusion. This was the psychology of dominance which the new advanced technology of armaments gave to the Western world. One can see it already in its first beginnings in the Indian Ocean when the Portuguese irrupted there and sank the Mecca pilgrim ships regardless of the age and sex of the passengers, and later when the British guns attacking in defence of the narcotics trade silenced the Wusung Forts. In a word – it does not matter what they think,

> ... for we have got
> the Maxim Gun, and they have not.

In this way Christendom was debauched by the fortuitous rise of the power of modern science and technology in its midst. Cultural and religious humility seemed to die, and still lie a-sleeping.

But the great movements of the world never have only the effects expected. Modern science, unlike the ethnically limited sciences of the medieval world, is intrinsically universal, sharing in the oecumenical oneness of mathematics but enormously more powerful. Slower in onset than the temporary lead of Europe but just as important came the realization of the Asian peoples that they too could share in all the benefits of modern science, they too could investigate the natural world in the new manner, could mark, read, learn and inwardly digest the *Journal of Biophysics* (for example), and regain their self-respect by achieving a standard of life as good as that of any other part of the world, while keeping all the best of their own cultural and religious traditions. The Renaissance in Europe, in which modern science arose, has been followed three centuries later by a Renaissance of Asia, and among its outstanding effects has been a revaluation and restoration of the great Asian religions. This is where cultural and religious humility is needed in the Western world today, and needed desperately.

For the dominance psychology is still at work. It was one thing for St Thomas to go to India in ancient times to preach the gospel unsupported by force, or for Ramon Lull, one of the most brilliant minds of the thirteenth century, to set sail as the representative of a culturally inferior society to try to convert the Muslims of the Maghrib. It was quite another thing for the missionaries in nineteenth-century China to behave with influence and authority in the knowledge that if they were withstood there were a couple of battalions of Western troops in the background ready to pressurize the provincial governor. Today the balance of power is quickly changing, but we Westerners are still the slaves of this idea that our culture and our religion is in some way 'superior' to those of our brothers and sisters in the great countries of Asia. I could find you examples in every issue of the weekly journals – only the other day there was Mr Arthur Koestler expatiating on the shortcomings of Indian and Japanese religion. Yet I should go so far as to say that this fixed idea is a cardinal danger to world peace. For 'he that despiseth Man, despiseth not Man but God'.

In the middle ages there were just rival convictions; no salvation outside Christendom and no quarter for those who challenged Christendom, no paradise outside Islam and no quarter for those who challenged Islam. But the injunction to the apostles to go and preach the gospel to all nations began to take on a different colour when modern science gave to their successors (for a time) the power to dominate all nations, as dominate them they did. Only now have the Muslim countries escaped from the political control of the 'unbelievers' (i.e. you and me). But they have remained faithful to their own religious heritage, and are now less likely than ever to exchange it for another. Is it not time that the rival convictions of the Middle Ages were replaced by a policy of greater fraternity, of mutual understanding between peoples, and much more humility on the part of western Christians – indeed must this not be so if man is to survive the destructive possibilities which modern physics and biology have placed in his hands?

A distinction may perhaps be made between the cultures of Africa and similar regions on the one hand and the civilizations of Asia on the other. There are some groups of mankind which before the advent of Christianity had never developed high forms of religious thought and feeling, and now they have no reason to give it up; likewise others adopted Islam and remain true to it. But the great civilizations of China and India have behind them a history of thought quite as extensive and at least as subtle and complex as that of Western Europe. You cannot really expect therefore that they will abandon their own traditional forms of thought and expression for those from a totally different culture. History shows us four great occasions on which China was offered the gift of organized Christianity, once in the eighth century when the Nestorians appeared from Syria, once in the thirteenth when Cambaluc (Peking) had a Franciscan archbishop, once again in the brilliant days of the seventeenth-century Jesuit mission, and lastly in the nineteenth century when the envoys of the Protestants opened hospitals and translated scientific textbooks. But the gift was always declined and today it must be said that organized Christianity has been decisively rejected by Chinese culture. The same is essentially true of Hindu and Muslim India. It is not merely (as is often recognized) that the Christian gospel and the Western way of life have all too frequently seemed inextricably bound together. Naturally every people should mould Christian customs in its own way, as for example at Vaddukoddai, in northern Ceylon, where I found the Book of Common Prayer combined with oil lamps and sitting on the floor. But matters go far deeper than this, and what Hebrew, Greek and Roman made of our Western Semitic–Hellenistic revelation can not only never now be imposed upon the Chinese and the Indian souls but will never be accepted by them in place of their own. In the light of this, is not most of the thinking still current about the dissemination of Christianity just wishful thinking? To assume the future extension of the visible organized Church to all mankind is unrealistic and pre-judges the purposes of God. But we are not as men without hope. If heaven is where the good are, and where good things are done, perhaps the invisible Church already covers the broad earth without our knowing it, most truly one spirit, under one God and Father of all. In the words of William Blake:

And All must love the human form
In heathen, Turk, or Jew:
Where Mercy, Love and Pity dwell
There God is dwelling too.

Christianity, like all other religions, is concerned with eternal values. Our presumption surely lies in expecting to find them everywhere incarnated in forms familiar to us. They are there in other forms, and these are forms which we must set ourselves to learn about. The working of the Holy Spirit and his righteousness must be sought for throughout the ages within social and cultural patterns unfamiliar to us, but with which we ought to make ourselves familiar. The refusal to do this is the presumptuousness, the spiritual wickedness, which is one of the worst features of Western culture. May it not be that the attempt to impose our theology and our philosophy and our conception of social order on others, without listening to what they have to say about the revelations vouchsafed unto them, is indeed one of the forms of the spirit of evil in things heavenly? Would it not be more Christian to try to learn instead of always assuming the right to teach? By all means let us expound *In principio erat verbum*, but hear and revere just as willingly *Tao kho Tao, fei chhang Tao*.

If we only knew the treasures of human experience of God contained in cultures which because we will not work to understand them seem so foreign to us, we should hug them to our breasts and cry out in amazement at the work of the Holy Spirit under all meridians.

... Divided all
In families we see our shadows born, and thence we know
That man subsists by brotherhood and universal love.
We fall on one another's necks, more closely we embrace.
Not for ourselves, but for the Eternal family we live.
Man liveth not by self alone, but in his brother's face
Each shall behold the Eternal Father and love and joy abound.

When once you look you can see the truth working itself out both in people and in books, embodied in traditions often more praiseworthy than our own. A few examples of these three things may be mentioned. First, among people, let us think of Hsimên Pao in 424 B.C. abolishing the sacrifice of girls to the God of the Yellow River; or the Buddhist pilgrim Hsüan-Chuang in A.D. 635 abominating the suicide temple which he found in India; or Su Chhiung the Confucian about A.D. 580 administering his province in one of the worst times of war, plague and famine, with all possible humanity and goodness, never wavering in his belief that if mankind would follow the counsels of the Sage the world could be a true co-operative commonwealth. In China you can see the staunch members of the Yü Shih Pu, the Censorate, courting death (and often receiving it) century after century rather than let maladministration and extortion in the provinces go unpunished. In India you can see one of the greatest of poets, Kabīr, mediating between the mutual hatreds of Hindu and Muslim. 'The tree bears not fruit for itself,' saith Kabīr, 'nor for itself does the stream collect its waters; for the benefit of others alone does the sage assume a bodily shape.'

Then there are the texts. Take for example one of the most central of Christian affirmations, that love 'seeketh not its own', and looks for no reward. Then read that great philosophical poem the *Tao Tê Ching*, the basic Taoist scripture. Concerning the Order of Nature, it says:

> The Supreme Tao, how it floods in every direction!
> This way and that, there is no place where it does not go.
> All things look to it for life, and it refuses none of them;
> Yet when its work is accomplished it possesses nothing.
> Clothing and nourishing all things, it does not lord it over them.
> Since it asks for nothing from them
> It may be classed among things of low estate;
> But since all things obey it without coercion
> It may be named Supreme.
> It does not arrogate greatness to itself
> And so it fulfils its Greatness.

Or again:

> How did the great rivers and seas get their kingship over the hundred
> lesser streams?

Through the merit of being lower than they; that was how they got their
   kingship.
Therefore the sage, in order to be above the people, |
Must speak as though he were lower than they.
In order to guide them
He must put himself behind them.
Thus when he is above, the people have no burden,
When he is ahead, they feel no hurt.
Thus everything under heaven is glad to be directed by him
And does not find his guidance irksome.

And a voice from India echoes the great doctrine.

The *Gita* stresses everywhere that the man who performs *svadharma* should
give up the fruit. One must act but one must also renounce the fruit. Water
the tree, tend it with care, but do not desire to enjoy its shade or its fruit or
flowers. This is *karma-yoga* through the practice of *svadharma*.

Such are the words of Acharya Vinoba Bhave, the great exponent
of Indian land reform. In the presence of such spirituality any
preoccupation with the details of Christian orthodoxy in which
we may happen to have been brought up is like turning the divine
guest away from our door.

Thirdly there is the evidence of history. Christians must not
only reconsider their belief that the whole world will necessarily
some day be matriculated in the ecclesiastical organization of
Christendom; they must give less grudging recognition to the
achievements of other peoples and other religions. The doctrine
of compassion in Buddhism was present beside that of world-
emptiness from the beginning, *karuna* was always at least the equal
of *sunya*. Its imagery might take forms curious to us; I have found
myself rapt in contemplation in the Tunhuang caves before that
picture of a Bodhisattva-King cutting a piece out of his own leg |
to feed a hungry bird. But the upshot was practical, and if you go
to the beautiful mountain abbey of Mihintale in Ceylon you will
find at its foot a large and elaborate hospital founded at the
beginning of the Christian era. Buddhism indeed has a certain
priority for the foundation of institutions of medical care. To the
Buddhists again we owe a cosmology far more open than that

prison of crystalline celestial spheres in which the medieval Christians lived. Before their era began the Buddhists were descanting on the millions of beings in a single drop of pond-water, and the thousands of years which it would take for a body to travel through space from one of the worlds to another. When we turn to Islam, all the accent is on brotherhood. No medieval society had better laws and customs concerning slavery. No religion in history can boast of having made brotherhood more real and actual in everyday life. In his last sermon, the Prophet told his people that excellence consisted only in deed ('By their works shall ye know them.') Pride of colour or race was utterly condemned. 'The Arab,' he said, 'is not superior to the non-Arab; the non-Arab is not superior to the Arab. You are all sons of Adam, and Adam was made of earth. Verily all Muslims are brothers. . . . If a deformed Abyssinian slave holds authority over you and leads you according to the Book of Allah, hear him and obey.' Nowhere has the true spirit of Islam been so tersely summarized as in the last speech of its founder. And what of Judaism? But one single word; a man said to Rabbi Hillel, 'Tell me the essence of Judaism while I stand on one leg!' To which he replied, 'Thou shalt love thy neighbour as thyself.' Let then the fact be faced – no people have had a monopoly of religious truth.

In this great endeavour of understanding we shall know we are getting on by the degree of empathy with which we can respond to truth in unfamiliar patterns of symbolism. It will not be given to all of us in person to burn incense to the ancestral culture-heroes of China, to discuss with those who revere the *lingam* and the *yoni*, or to light a candle at the tomb of Maimonides. But we can all make an effort to 'get outside our own skins', to cultivate friends of other civilizations, and to learn to respond to the numinous in their great traditions. I will submit you to a little test in this regard. In a recent publication there appeared a poem from which I quote the following verses:

> When he was seventy and growing frail
> The teacher after all felt the need for peace,
> For once again in the country kindness did not prevail

And malice once again was on the increase.
So he tied his shoe-lace . . .

But before the fourth day's rocky travelling was done,
A customs man interposed his authority.
'Please declare your valuables' – 'None.'
And the boy leading the ox said, 'A teacher, you see.'
That met the contingency.

But the man, cheerful, and struck by a sudden notion,
Went on to ask, 'Who discovered something, you'd say?'
The boy replied, 'That yielding water in motion
Gets the better in the end of granite and porphyry,
You see, the hard thing gives way . . .'

And so the customs man asked the sage to write down his teaching, which he did in eighty-one very short chapters. I dare say no one present has noticed anything, no one has responded as they respond to a Christmas carol, for example. But I did when I first read it, for I knew that the teacher was Li Tan, Lao Tzu, riding away into the western mountains, and the customs man was Kuan Yin Tzu – legendary characters if you like, but legendary characters have a habit of having been quite real people. And the eighty-one chapters were those of the *Tao Tê Ching*. And Taoist wisdom is among the best of wisdoms, and Taoist temples among the most beautiful of all religious buildings the world over.

Lastly I have one or two caveats to make. What I have said is, I know, very easily misunderstood. It has nothing to do with Comtism or with Theosophy, or any other of those artificial mixtures or syncretic brews of religious experience. Every man is born into a social environment with a particular religion. Since religion is one of the great forms of human experience, he cannot be a full person unless he participates (critically, of course) in the religious practices of that matrix. But this he should do in such a way as to make him more percipient, more sensitive, more understanding, in relation to the traditional social-religious environments of other human beings with whom he may come in contact or of whom he may know. Secondly, in what I have said there is no *arrière-pensée* whatever of union in the face of challenge. It has, as you are aware, been said that the reunion of the Churches will take place in the last ditch of opposition to world communism, and only there; so also I might be supposed to be advocating a world union of faiths. This is far indeed from my thought. All forms of socialism and communism themselves derive profoundly (like certain much older doctrines such as Confucianism) from the determination to build (in our phraseology) the Kingdom of God on earth, and theological religion, whether transcendental or immanentist, will settle its accounts with them in due course. What I am pleading for is the mutual understanding of the great civilizations by each other; meanwhile the wind of collectivist humanism is rising to purge and purify them all. This mutual understanding is the recognition that all mankind is one body and one spirit, under one God and Father supreme. And this recognition implies that men of every culture shall go and sit down in the lowest room, and give over exalting themselves as sole possessors of all truth.

I will end these thoughts by quoting to you a Sufic poem of Akbar's historian Abū'l Faẓl 'Allāmī (1551–1602), a man who lived, like Galileo, in the generation just after John Caius. It echoes those words with which this talk began – 'one God and Father of all' –

> O God, in every temple I find people that seek thee
> In every language I hear spoken, people praise thee!
>> Hinduism and Islam both feel after thee,
>> Each religion says: 'Thou art one, without equal.'
> If it be a mosque, people murmur the holy prayer,
> And in the church, people ring the bell from love to thee.
>> Sometimes I frequent the Christian cloister and sometimes the mosque,
>> But it is thou whom I search for from temple to temple.
> Thine elect have no dealings with heresy or orthodoxy;
> For neither of these stands behind the screen of thy truth.
>> Speculation to the heretic, theology to the orthodox
>> But the dust of the rose-petal belongs to the heart of the perfume-seller.

CHRONOLOGY OF CHINA

		B.C.
	HSIA kingdom (legendary?)	c. 2000/c. 1500
	SHANG (YIN) kingdom	c. 1500/c. 1030
Chou Dynasty (Feudal Age)	Early Chou period	c. 1030/722
	Chhun Chhiu period	722/480
	Warring States period	480/221
	CHHIN dynasty	221/207
	HAN dynasty	A.D.
First unification	Earlier or Western Han	202 B.C./A.D. 9
	Hsin interregnum	9/23
	Later or Eastern Han	25/220
	Three Kingdoms period (San Kuo)	
First partition	Shu (west)	221/264
	Wei (north)	220/265
	Wu (south-east)	222/277
	CHIN dynasty	
Second unification	Western	265/317
	Eastern	317/420
	Former (or Liu) SUNG dynasty	420/479
	Northern Wei dynasty (Tho-Pa Tartar) later split into Eastern and Western	386/554
	Northern and Southern empires (Nan Pei Chhao)	479/581
	Chhi (southern)	479/502
Second partition	LIANG	502/557
	Chhen	557/581
	Chhi (northern)	550/581
	Chou (southern)	557/581
Third unification	SUI dynasty	581/618
	THANG dynasty	618/906
	Five Dynasty period (Wu Tai)	907/960
	Later Liang	907/923
Third partition	Later Thang	923/936
	Later Chin	936/946
	Later Han	947/950
	Later Chou	951/960

	Liao dynasty (Chhi-Tan Mongol)	A.D. 907/1125
	Hsi-Hsia State	990/1227
Fourth unification	Northern SUNG dynasty	960/1126
Fourth partition	Southern SUNG dynasty	1127/1279
	Chin (Ju-Chen Tartar) dynasty	1125/1234
	YUAN (Mongol) dynasty	1260/1368
Fifth unification	MING dynasty	1368/1644
	CHHING (Manchu) dynasty	1644/1911
	Republic	1912/1949
	People's Republic	1949

INDEX

Index

INDEX

Individualism, among Chinese scholars and thinkers, 58
Indo-Ceylonese culture, 176 ff
Indo-China, 18
Indoctrination, 51
Indonesia, 165
  inventions, 20
Industrial Revolution, 29
Industrialization, 29, 35–7, 53, 79, 169
  without capitalism, 167
Inertia, 181
Inquisition, See Holy Inquisition
Instincts, 180
Institutions of learning, 135–6, 142 ff
Integrative levels, 27, 67, 95–6, 194
Intellectuals
  and Communism, 45, 66
  and dialectical materialism, 71, 156
  and the Kuomintang, 45
  and the mandarinate, 35
  and manual work, 47–8
Internal combustion engine, 87
International co-operation, 97
International law, See Law
Iron Bureaux, 43–4
Iron-casting, 16, 44, 84, 155
Iron industry, 'nationalization' of, 43–4
Iron-workers, 106
Ironsides, 64
Irrigation and conservancy works, 42–3, 47
Isaiah, 141–2, 145
Islam, 12, 17 (1), 25, 74, 75 (1), 168, 203–4, 208
  learned institutions, 136
Israel, 15, 26, 34, 60, 62, 64, 69, 75 (1), 141, 208

Japan, and the Japanese, 40, 54, 60, 144, 164, 171
  religion, 203
Jātaka birth-stories, 138, 176 ff
Jen min kung shê ('communes'), 59
Jesuits, 35, 71, 76, 86, 108, 156–7, 204
  and modern science, 13 (1), 77
  translations of Confucian classics by, 90, 107
Jews, 74, 196
Jones, Sir William, 136–7
Journals, 61
Judaism, See Israel
Julius Caesar (Shakespeare), 70

Jurisprudence, See Law
Justinian, Code of, See Code of Justinian

Kabir (Indian poet), 27, 206
Kan Ying (Han official and traveller), 20 (1)
Kansu, 166
Karma ('spiritual heritage'), 180
Karuna (compassion), 66, 177, 193, 207
Kemal, Yusuf, 35 (1)
Khang Tshang Tzu (Book of Master Khang Tshang), 180
Khang Yu-Wei (writer, 1884), 78
Khwarizmi, al-, Muhammad (ninth-century A.D. Persian algebraist), 143
King, F. H., 46 (1)
'Kingdom of God on earth', 64, 141, 210
Knights of St John, 115
Knowledge, theory of, 20–1, 92
Ko Lao Hui (secret society), 57
Koestler, Arthur, 203
Korea, and Koreans, 18, 28, 164, 167, 171
Korean war, 40, 147 ff, 171
Koshas (envelopes), 180
Ku Kung Po Wu Kuan. See Imperial Palace Museum
Kuan pu nai tê ong ('the old gentleman of the irrigated garden who attained [peace] through forbearance'), 53
Kuan Tzu, 92
Kuan Yin Tzu (legendary character), 209
Kuei Thien Lu, 46
Kungshu Phan (artisan), 64
Kunming, 152
Kuo Mo-Jo (archaeologist and ancient historian), 65
Kuo Tzu Chien, See College of the Sons of the Nation
Kuomintang, 36, 38, 45, 54, 65, 79, 80, 167
Kuomintang troops, American airlift of, 23 (2)

Labour Govenment, 163
Lacquer, 19
Lamaist Buddhism, 164
Lao Tzu (philosopher), 26, 91, 209
Large-family ethos, 52–4
Latin Church, 177

Index

INDEX

223